The High School Student's Guide to Writing A Great Research Paper

101 Easy Tips & Tricks to Make Your Work Stand Out

BY ERIKA EBY

The High School Student's Guide to Writing A Great Research Paper:

101 Easy Tips & Tricks to Make Your Work Stand Out

Copyright © 2013 by Atlantic Publishing Group, Inc.
1210 SW 23rd Place • Ocala, Florida 34471 • 800-814-1132 • Fax 352-622-1875
Website: www.atlantic-pub.com • Email: sales@atlantic-pub.com
SAN Number: 268-1250

Library of Congress Cataloging-in-Publication Data
Eby, Erika, 1988-
   The high school student's guide to writing a great research paper : 101 easy tips & tricks to make your work stand out / Erika Eby.
      p. cm.
   Includes bibliographical references and index.
   ISBN 978-1-60138-604-5 (alk. paper) -- ISBN 1-60138-604-4 (alk. paper) 1. English language--Composition and exercises--Study and teaching (Secondary) 2. Report writing--Study and teaching (Secondary) 3. Research--Methodology--Study and teaching (Secondary) I. Title.
   LB1631.E33 2012
   428.0071'2--dc23
                                2011046665

BOOK PRODUCTION DESIGN: T.L. Price • design@tlpricefreelance.com   Printed on Recycled Paper

Printed in the United States

A few years back we lost our beloved pet dog Bear, who was not only our best and dearest friend but also the "Vice President of Sunshine" here at Atlantic Publishing. He did not receive a salary but worked tirelessly 24 hours a day to please his parents.

Bear was a rescue dog who turned around and showered myself, my wife, Sherri, his grandparents Jean, Bob, and Nancy, and every person and animal he met (well, maybe not rabbits) with friendship and love. He made a lot of people smile every day.

We wanted you to know a portion of the profits of this book will be donated in Bear's memory to local animal shelters, parks, conservation organizations, and other individuals and nonprofit organizations in need of assistance.

– Douglas & Sherri Brown

PS: We have since adopted two more rescue dogs: first Scout, and the following year, Ginger. They were both mixed golden retrievers who needed a home.

Want to help animals and the world? Here are a dozen easy suggestions you and your family can implement today:

- *Adopt and rescue a pet from a local shelter.*
- *Support local and no-kill animal shelters.*
- *Plant a tree to honor someone you love.*
- *Be a developer — put up some birdhouses.*
- *Buy live, potted Christmas trees and replant them.*
- *Make sure you spend time with your animals each day.*
- *Save natural resources by recycling and buying recycled products.*
- *Drink tap water, or filter your own water at home.*
- *Whenever possible, limit your use of or do not use pesticides.*
- *If you eat seafood, make sustainable choices.*
- *Support your local farmers market.*
- *Get outside. Visit a park, volunteer, walk your dog, or ride your bike.*

Five years ago, Atlantic Publishing signed the Green Press Initiative. These guidelines promote environmentally friendly practices, such as using recycled stock and vegetable-based inks, avoiding waste, choosing energy-efficient resources, and promoting a no-pulping policy. We now use 100-percent recycled stock on all our books. The results: in one year, switching to post-consumer recycled stock saved 24 mature trees, 5,000 gallons of water, the equivalent of the total energy used for one home in a year, and the equivalent of the greenhouse gases from one car driven for a year.

Table of Contents

Chapter 8: Writing The Introduction 161

Chapter 9: Writing the Body of Your Paper 181

Chapter 10: Wrapping Things Up, The Conclusion 203

Chapter 11: Formatting and Reference Pages 217

Introduction

Let me set the scene for you: It is getting late on Sunday night, and you should be in bed. You have school early the next morning. You know you should have started your research paper sooner, but you were floundering and not sure what to do. There were also community events, friend and family obligations, extracurricular activities, and other homework to occupy your time all weekend.

Now, here you sit, staring at an intimidatingly empty white word document waiting for you to fill it. The cursor is pulsing. The clock is ticking. And you are panicking. Sound familiar?

This is a scenario that every high school student faces at some point. I know it happened to me more than once during my high school career. Add in technical difficulties and stress from hormones, friends, and sports, and you have a tempest of trouble brewing. Stress, anxiety, and writer's block all are soon to follow. It's easy to convince yourself that writing a paper should be a piece of cake, but according to the National Center for Education Statistics, four out of five students are not proficient writers.

If you need inspiration and motivation for writing your next paper, this book can be the catalyst you need to get started. It can also be the helping hand you need to walk you through the process of putting together a fresh, original paper that is so loaded with extensive vocabulary, smooth transitions, and concise details that teachers won't want to lay a red pen on it.

I wrote my share of last-minute papers in high school. Sometimes I would be truly inspired and manage to throw together something that would impress teachers. More often, I would flounder around at my desk for a few hours before throwing something together out of desperation. For that reason, I have tried to make this the book that I wish I would have had in high school. Not a dry rundown of writing procedures and grammar lessons (though there will be some grammar covered, so get your groans out of the way now), but a useful guide with the modern high school student in mind.

I interviewed students and teachers to get several perspectives to add to my own in order to make this book something students would actually want to use. In this book, you will learn every aspect of the research paper and its writing process from dissecting the prompt and figuring out precisely what your teacher is looking for, to ending with a flourish that will set your paper apart from the rest.

With the 101 tips and tricks in this book, you will learn how to develop clever, new topics as well as how to compose a helpful and organized outline before you begin writing. You will learn how to brainstorm myriad subjects that your teacher will want to read and learn how to articulate them smoothly and easily in your paper. Also, you will find out how to keep the same flow and tone throughout every paragraph.

Got writer's block? This book shares tricks for overcoming this obstacle every time, as well as how to get over procrastination, how to cope with problems like dyslexia, how to avoid plagiarism, and how to find the best research sources, both online and off. If you need to write and cite in a certain style, this book will give you the details you need to get your Works Cited page organized in perfect form.

Even when you reach the editing, proofing, and revising stages of your paper, this book will walk you through every step and offer easy, simple pieces of advice that you will remember for life. Learn all the finishing touches and find out every detail you need for turning in your complete, eye-catching draft, including double-spacing, margins, alignment, and title pages.

So fasten your seatbelts and get ready for a ride through writing a paper you can be proud of.

CHAPTER 1:

Before You Begin

Whether research papers are something you have seldom had to deal with thus far in your academic career or you have been writing them for a while, there are a few important things to consider before diving into the writing process. Research papers come in all shapes and sizes, so understanding exactly what you are getting yourself into when starting a paper is crucial. The following sections offer some basic information to consider as you begin the process of writing a research paper.

What is a Research Paper?

The majority of papers you will write in an academic setting will be research papers. Any paper requiring the writer to research a particular topic is, by definition, a research paper. Unlike essays, which are often based largely on opinion and written from the author's point of view, research papers are based in fact. Anecdotes and creative storytelling have no place inside a research paper. This is not to say research papers cannot be creative and do not contain the author's opinion. They should be, and they do. The big difference between a research paper and many other forms of writing is that research papers force writers to back up their opinions and assertions with facts found through thorough research on a given topic. They force students to form an opinion on a topic, research that topic, and then showcase that knowledge by writing about it.

Many students make the mistake of thinking that if they avoid taking English or "Writing Intensive" classes, they will not have to write research papers. If you fall into this category, prepare to be surprised. True, in an English class you will likely have to write several papers, and most high schools require students to take a certain number of composition classes. It does not end there, though. History classes might require you to research on WWII or Ancient Greece and write about it. Government or Economics classes can assign papers about current events or matters of government policy. Chemistry or Physics may require you to write a final project about a famous scientist or the development of an important scientific theory. Research papers come in all shapes and sizes, and they will only become more prevalent in college. If you can grasp the basics now, you will be that much more prepared down the road.

Tip No. 1
Research papers force you to form an opinion on a topic and then back it up with facts.

You can try to be creative in your presentation, but at the end of the day, do not forget that research papers rely on facts found through research to construct a logical and compelling argument. Therefore, your facts must be solid, or you will not have a solid foundation on which to base your opinion.

Types of Research Papers

There are several types of research papers. Some research papers are short, and some are in-depth. Everything from writing a three-page literary analysis to writing a detailed semester-long project is a type of research paper. The beauty of research papers is that whether you are writing a summary of scientific research done over the course of a semester, analyzing a novel, or drawing conclusions from several psychological studies, they all follow the same basic structure. The tips found in this book can apply to any research paper you find yourself writing.

Tip No. 2   Research papers of all types have almost identical structures at their core.

There will be some basic differences, but if you can write one type of research paper, you can write another. Do not let literary criticism intimidate you if your favorite subject is chemistry, or scientific research scare you if you have barely glanced at a periodic table.

Although the same basic structure and tips can be applied to just about any research paper, some stylistic rules will vary from subject to subject. Being familiar with MLA format will help you with that English paper, but it might not help with a chemistry analysis.

Tip No. 3   Familiarize yourself with different formats for writing papers.

Avoid going overboard, but having a passing knowledge of multiple styles will make them much less intimidating if you happen to run across them at a later date.

Questions to Ask Before Starting a Paper

Now that you have a solid understanding of exactly what a research paper is, it is important to make sure you have all of the information you need to write the best possible research paper for a given assignment.

Often, teachers will give out a rubric or assignment sheet with all of the information you need to know about an assignment, but this is not always the case.

Tip No.

4 **Do not put off reading over assignments for research papers.** There are few things worse than ignoring a huge project until the last minute and then realizing you do not understand part of it. Often, it is too late to get clarification at that point, so read those assignment sheets immediately upon receiving them.

Sometimes you do not receive a clear list of instructions. This can be especially frustrating for students as they flounder through an assignment, completely unsure of what is expected of them or whether they are even doing the assignment correctly. Asking your teacher for clarification on specific points before starting an assignment will save you a lot of fuss and headache later in the writing process. Your teachers likely have regular office hours, generally before and after school, or may host special study or Q&A sessions. You can also see if your teacher would be willing to meet with you during a study hall or at another convenient time.

If all else fails and your teacher is unavailable, your classmates can often help. One advantage in a high school setting is the ease with which you can find a student in the same class, or who has taken the same class previously. An older friend or sibling may have taken the same class previously, possibly even with the same teacher, and they can likely clarify any questions you might have. Many schools also have tutors or writing centers available to help students with papers, so use these resources to your advantage. Always check the class syllabus or website, if possible, to determine whether there is any additional information there.

> **Tip No. 5 Ask questions about an assignment until you are sure you have a handle on it.**
>
> Many students needlessly lose points on assignments simply because they did not understand every aspect of it. Ask questions, get clarification, and do not wait until the last minute to do it. You might find that help is unavailable then, when it would have been earlier.

The following is a list of questions to ask either yourself or your teacher before beginning any paper:

- **Are there any requirements for the topic of the paper?** Often, teachers will provide a general theme for an assignment, and students are expected to pick a topic relating to that theme.

- **Are there any subjects that are off-limits for this paper?** Sometimes, a teacher might simply say one or two topics covered within the class should not be included in any papers. They might also have a list of topics that they see too often and recommend that students avoid.

■ **How long should the paper be?** This is fairly important because the length of a paper will change what types of topics you can adequately cover within the assignment. Some teachers will not give a set length for an assignment, but most will at least give a ballpark page or word count. Make sure you have this information so you can plan the paper accordingly.

■ **What format should the paper be in?** There are several different styles or formats in which to write a paper. Be sure you know what format your teacher is expecting to receive the paper in so you can brush up on the appropriate format.

■ **Is there a required number of sources?** Sometimes teachers will set a minimum number of sources for a paper or just have a rough expectation of how many sources are appropriate for a research paper. Getting docked points for not having the proper number of sources is a petty thing to lose points over, so make sure you are aware of any requirements and choose a topic that lets you meet them.

■ **Are there any types of sources that are restricted?** Teachers might restrict certain types of sources for a given assignment. Most commonly, teachers will restrict the number or type of Internet sources used in an assignment, but sometimes, other restrictions can apply, so always ask.

■ **Are there any additional materials that should be turned in with the paper?** Some assignments might require you to turn in multiple drafts of the same paper, turn in a cover page or an outline, or include a certain number of charts or graphs with your paper. Most teachers will make this clear when this is the case, but always ask for clarification if you have any questions so you know you are turning in the correct materials.

- **Does the teacher have any other specific requirements for the paper?** Every teacher is different, and often, they have their own requirements for how they want things done. They might require you to print your paper in a specific font or print your pages double-sided. Usually, when teachers have odd or specific non-standard expectations for papers, they will make them clear in the class syllabus or on an assignment sheet, but always ask for clarification if you have any doubt or are confused.

Study Guide

❏ Research papers are a staple of any academic discipline.

❏ Research papers require students to form an opinion on a topic and then back up their assertions about the subject with facts found through research.

❏ Although different types of research papers might require different formats and will cover varying subjects, much of the basic structure and the tips for improvement are universal.

❏ Because there are many things to consider when writing a research paper, do not be afraid to ask questions and get all of the important information you need before you begin writing and researching.

❏ Use all of the resources your school has available if you are having trouble understanding an assignment and your teacher is unavailable.

CHAPTER 2:

Sentences and Paragraphs

Many students roll their eyes when the nuts and bolts of writing get mentioned. Some feel it is boring, while others feel that it is simply too easy. It might come as a bit of a shock to know that most students are not able to correctly write in a language that they can speak fluently. This is not a statement about illiteracy. The fact is that written English is not the same as spoken English. This means, at its core, if you are writing your paper the same way you would speak about it, you are probably making mistakes.

When speaking, it is not necessary to point out where there are commas, periods, and paragraph breaks. Your audience can infer your meaning based on tone of voice, body language, and other cues. Because of this, spoken English is usually much more informal than written English. Speaking in fragments or run-on sentences is commonplace. When writing, however, this is unacceptable. Because of this, the following sections will discuss the basics of sentence and paragraph structure.

What is a Sentence?

At its core, a sentence is a string of words that forms a complete thought. Sentences are made up of one or more clauses. Clauses consist of a stated or implied subject, a predicate, and a preposition. Words like 'predicate' and 'verb' scare a lot of students because they make grammar sound complicated and confusing. Predicate is really just a fancy word for whatever it is you are trying to say about the subject of the sentence. Likewise, verb is a fancy way of saying "a word that shows the relationship between the subject and the predicate."

Sentence Structure Explained

Trying to memorize all the parts of speech is useful, but it can also be confusing. If you struggle with sentence diagrams in English class, these examples should help.

Example sentence: When Billy plays baseball, he is always the team's pitcher.

This sentence consists of two clauses:

1. When Billy plays baseball
2. He is always the team's pitcher.

Each clause has its own subject. The sentence is about Billy, so he is the subject. In the first clause "Billy" is the subject and in the second clause the pronoun "he" is the subject.

Each clause also shows what Billy is doing, or what his relationship to something is. What does Billy do?

Billy:

- "plays baseball"
- "is always the pitcher"

These are the basics of sentence structure. Now try to take one of your own sentences and do the same thing.

If you are already confused, do not get discouraged. You do not have to remember all of the parts of a sentence to be able to write a good sentence. Just remember three basic concepts:

1.) A sentence should be a complete thought.

2.) A sentence needs a subject.

3.) In order to have a complete sentence you need to say something about the subject and show how that something is linked to the subject.

The parts of speech can be confusing and it seems like a lot to remember. If sentence structure is something you have trouble with, mark the sections of whatever writing guide your school uses that deal with parts of speech. If your school does not use a writing guide, add the Purdue OWL (**www. owl.english.purdue.edu**) to your bookmarks.

Common Sentence Problems

Now that you understand what a sentence is, this section will spend some time discussing the most common problems or errors students make when writing sentences.

Comma splices

A comma splice is possibly the most common grammatical error in written English. A comma splice occurs when a comma is used to link two independent clauses. Once you know what a comma splice is, they are fairly easy to spot because the clause before the comma and the clause after the comma will both work as stand-alone sentences. For example "I hit the ball, I scored a home run." is a comma splice. "I hit the ball" and "I scored a home run" are both sentences in and of themselves. You can correct this error by adding a conjunction (in this case "and") after the comma. You could also change the comma to a period and make two separate sentences. Changing the comma to a semicolon is also an option.

So the correct sentences would be:

"I hit the ball, and I scored a home run."

"I hit the ball. I scored a home run."

"I hit the ball; I scored a home run."

Fused/run-on sentences

A fused sentence, also known as a run-on sentence, is basically a comma splice without the comma. A fused sentence consists of two complete clauses that are thrown into the same sentence without any punctuation to separate them. So "I hit the ball I scored a home run" would be an example of this. Fused sentences have a tendency to become comma splices because students see that there is an error and do not know how to fix it, so they use a comma. Fused sentences should be fixed the same way as comma splices.

Sentence fragments

Sentence fragments are exactly what they sound like. A sentence fragment is an incomplete thought that is written as a standalone sentence. These can be fixed by either combining the fragment with another clause to make it a complete thought or by removing words from the fragment that link it to another non-exist ant sentence. For example, the fragment "Because I hit the home run" could be corrected to "We won the game because I hit the home run" or "I hit the home run."

Subject/verb and tense agreement

Another common error students make is improper subject/verb agreement. What this means is that the verb used in the sentence does not match the subject of the sentence. Usually this is either because the wrong tense is used or the wrong plural/singular form of a word is used. For example: "My brothers is at school" is incorrect. "Brothers" is plural, while "is" is singular. "I run four miles last week" is incorrect. The sentence is in the past tense, but "run" is a present tense verb.

Active and Passive Voice

You may have already heard a teacher discuss active and passive voice. Regardless of whether you have or have not, understanding the two and when they are appropriate can be tricky at first.

- Active voice shows the subject of the sentence taking an action.
  - "The boy hit the ball."
- Passive voice shows the SUBJECT of the sentence being acted upon.
  - "The ball was hit by the boy."

As a general rule, almost everything you write should be in the active voice. The active voice is less confusing to readers. They know from the beginning of the sentence what the subject is doing. Generally speaking, the person or thing taking the action is the most important part of the sentence.

Active or Passive?

Some students (and even teachers!) confuse using the past tense, or using a "to be" verb (is, am, are, was, were, be, etc.) with being passive. This is not true, so do not make this mistake!

A sentence being active or passive is about more than just verb choice or when the action was performed. Just because a sentence uses word "is" or "was" does not mean it is a passive sentence.

Example:

Passive: "Baseball was what Sally wanted to play."

Active: "Sally wanted to play baseball"

Here is a quick test to tell if a sentence is active or passive. First, find the thing in the sentence that is performing the action. Now check to see where in the sentence it is. If the thing doing the action is at the beginning of the sentence, then it is active. If the thing doing the acting is later in the sentence, or not mentioned in the sentence at all, then it is most likely passive.

There are, however, exceptions to the active-only rule. Usually they occur when the person or thing taking the action is not important to the point the writer is making. This is the case is scientific writing much of the time because the reaction or result of a procedure or experiment is the focus, rather than the individual who started the experiment. Likewise, when describing a circumstance in which someone is a victim or when the subject is not known, the active voice is usually more appropriate. For example "Sarah's car was vandalized" is an acceptable use of passive voice.

What is a Paragraph?

A paragraph is a string of sentences that all focus on a single topic. A cohesive paragraph functions much the same way a cohesive sentence does, just on a larger scale. A paragraph should introduce a subject and then discuss something about that subject in a coherent and organized way. A good paragraph is easy for readers to follow, but a bad paragraph can ruin an entire paper by confusing the point the writer was trying to make. You can have the best ideas in the world, but if you cannot present them in a way that makes sense, you will not get far.

Basic Paragraphing

The rule of thumb for writing paragraphs is simple. One idea should equal one paragraph. If you start introducing a new idea, then start a new paragraph. If you begin to transition into a new idea, it belongs in a new paragraph. This is not to say you cannot have supporting details for your paragraph's main point. If your support gets so long that it turns into its own topic, however, it belongs in its own paragraph.

Elements of a paragraph

A paragraph needs to have all of the following elements in order to be effective: a topic sentence, a unified and coherent progression, supporting details, and an ending transition.

A topic sentence starts the paragraph and should explain what the point of your paragraph will be. If at any point you wonder if you should start a new paragraph, look at your topic sentence. If what you are saying does not fit with the topic sentence, it should be in a different paragraph. By doing this you will ensure your paragraphs are unified and cohesive.

A paragraph also needs to have adequate support. If it helps, jot down the topic of your paragraph and then write a word or two to represent each supporting idea you have for that topic. A good paragraph should have at least three supporting details. Longer or more in-depth pieces may have more than this, but three is a good number to shoot for. If you cannot come up with three supporting details, you will either need to do more research or adjust your topic sentence accordingly.

Lastly, make sure to include proper transitions in your paragraphs. Transitions are linking statements that occur at the beginning and endings of paragraphs so that the ideas presented in them flow together smoothly. If you switch immediately from talking about one idea to discussing something completely different, the readers will mentally stumble as they try to follow along. Transitions give readers a heads up that the topic is changing and help them absorb more of the point.

Example Paragraph:

Creating an anti-hero is much harder than creating a hero, but it is also much more rewarding (at least in my humble opinion). There is a fine line between a character being lovably wicked or just appalling. Heroes, on the other hand, are easy. They always take the high ground. The writer can program in a set of morals and values, wind the hero up, and let him or her go. Heroes can get away with being flat and stale as cardboard. Not to say that all heroes are — plenty are not — but as long as they perform heroic acts, they are still a hero regardless of character depth. A flat anti-hero, however, is usually just a villain. In order to walk the fine grey line, anti-heroes need to be complex and well developed. They need to have justifiable reasons for their actions, well-developed intentions, and something that makes them feel "real." All important characters should be developed until they have that breath of life — you add details drop by drop until finally the cup overflows with a personality all its own, but anti-heroes need that quality in order to be likable.

Study Guide

❏ Sentences and paragraphs are the building blocks of a paper.

  ❏ Sentences are strings of words.
  ❏ Paragraphs are strings of sentences.

❏ Familiarize yourself with the most common sentence errors, which are:

  ❏ Comma splices
  ❏ Run-on/fused sentences
  ❏ Fragments
  ❏ Tense and subject/verb agreement

❏ Sentences are made up of clauses.

❏ Clauses must have a subject and a verb.

❏ Sentences should almost always be active instead of passive.

  ❏ An active sentence has the subject performing an action.
  ❏ A passive sentence has the subject being acted upon.

❏ A paragraph is a group of sentences that work together to explain an idea or concept. All sentences in a paragraph should relate to the same topic.

❏ A paragraph should begin with a topic sentence that explains what the paragraph is about.

❏ If your paragraph covers multiple topics, break it down into smaller paragraphs.

❏ A paragraph should end with a transition to link it to the next idea in the paper.

CHAPTER 3:

Prewriting and Getting Started

Most students let out a collective groan whenever "prewriting" for an assignment is mentioned. For whatever reason, sitting down and writing to get ideas is a huge turnoff for many students. Few realize how vital this step is to the writing process, and then they wonder why they keep getting stuck when it comes time to sit down and crank out that paper. Often, students feel like they were brimming over with ideas mere hours before while they were mulling over their assignments, but when it comes time to actually write the words down in a neat and coherent manner, nothing comes out. This is where prewriting comes in and exactly why it is so important to the writing process. Prewriting gets all those loose ideas down on paper, so they can be organized and do not wind up forgotten when it comes time to begin writing.

Myths about Prewriting

Tip No. 6 Do not dismiss prewriting.
Prewriting is a vital part of the writing process and a great way to generate and organize ideas so you do not forget them. Prewrite, at least a little bit, before any research paper.

The most common myth about prewriting is probably that it is not necessary and that it takes extra time students cannot afford to give up. Many students have a false concept of what it means to prewrite, which is why they so quickly dismiss it. The human thought process is disorganized and nebulous. Without prewriting, rather than having nice neat thoughts around which to structure a paper, students have to sort through all of these chaotic ideas while they are trying to write. This is difficult and only creates more work for students. The time you lose prewriting will be more than made up for with time not spent staring at your computer wondering what to write next.

Tip No. **7** **Prewriting saves time. It does not waste it.**
It can be tempting to say you do not have time to prewrite, but remember that prewriting will help you select a topic more quickly and will help you sort through the mess of ideas in your head, which will save time down the road.

Another common myth is that prewriting needs to be "good" or "organized." This is not the case. Several methods of prewriting exist, but the entire idea behind prewriting is to get ideas and concepts down on paper, whether good or bad. Once all of these rough notes are written down, they can be organized for later. Bad ideas can always be tossed out, and often, what seems to be a bad or useless idea can actually spark an idea or thought that turns into a great basis for a paper.

Tip No. **8** **Do not be afraid to let your prewriting be messy.**
This is not the paper yet, and the time for neatness will come later. Right now, it is more important to get those ideas on paper.

Students might also have tried one particular method of prewriting that they did not find helpful, so they dismiss prewriting as "not for them." The truth is there are as many types of prewriting as there are types of students. In this chapter, three common methods will be discussed, but students should feel free to experiment and find what works best for them. You might find that your prewriting needs more or less structure to it. You can combine prewriting methods or make up your own entirely, but this chapter will give you some ideas for what should be accomplished.

Tip No. 9 **Experiment with your prewriting.**
Find what works for you. One of the methods discussed in this book might work great, but it is possible that none of them really resonate with you. There are no right or wrong methods here, so experiment until you find something you can relate to and benefit from.

Benefits of prewriting

The ultimate goal of prewriting is to save time and frustration later during the writing process. Prewriting allows writers to quickly write down a large quantity of ideas to later be organized into a solid paper topic. Prewriting allows students to narrow down their paper topics from broad ideas to specifics, as well as figure out what key points to address within those specific ideas. Writers who do some sort of prewriting activity are less likely to get stuck while typing out the bulk of their papers. They are also much less likely to forget ideas they had planned to include in their papers.

Prewriting is especially useful when dealing with broad or ambiguous research assignments. Sometimes, classes will assign fairly specific topics for research papers but often assignments are general. For example, "Research something covered this semester in ancient history, and write a five- to seven-page paper on it," might be the assignment your teacher gives you. In instances such as this, students often have a few ideas of things that might be interesting but no direction when they sit down to begin researching or writing. Prewriting will help you generate a topic and often give you ideas for backup topics in case your research reveals a problem with your original idea.

> **Tip No. 10** Prewriting can help you choose a topic and give you ideas for what to write about that topic.
>
> We will discuss narrowing a topic down more in the next chapter, but prewriting is a great way to both figure out what topics would work best for your paper and determine how ideas within that topic are connected, which will form the basis for your paper.

On top of all of that, prewriting often allows students to make connections between ideas that they otherwise would not have. These connections are the stuff that excellent research papers are made of. Many papers on similar topics tend to cover the same points and read much alike, so any uncommon ideas you come up with will make your paper more interesting than the majority of the papers other students submit. Unique, well-thought-out ideas are the first step in getting out of the slush pile of papers on your teacher's desk.

Tip No. 11 Embrace creative thinking and unique ideas at this stage.
You never know what will turn into a great research paper, so embrace strange ideas or connections between topics as they come to you. These unique ideas can turn into great papers your teacher will enjoy reading.

Mind-Mapping or Clustering

As was stated previously, human thought patterns are nebulous and not neatly organized. The mind's filing system is not alphabetical or chronological. Exactly how the mind groups memories is not fully understood, but things are grouped much closer to categorically.

Often, our minds make connections between ideas or events in what seems like random ways.

Tip No. 12 Even if your thoughts seem organized, they are not.
Often, when people do not have a computer or notebook handy and are mulling over ideas, there seem to be many of them and they seem to flow neatly together. In actuality, they are nebulous and loosely connected. Mind-mapping takes advantage of this by making a web of ideas that visually approximates how your ideas are connected in your mind.

Mind-mapping or clustering takes advantage of this fact by helping you visually lay out concepts and ideas as you think of them in an organic, non-hierarchical way. Many students are already familiar with this technique, though they might have heard it referred to as idea mapping, web diagramming, or something similar. These charts are not only helpful in organizing large amounts of information, but also in bringing together words and visual aids. For this reason, visual learners generally find this method of prewriting particularly effective.

Visual, web-like connection of ideas

Starting a mind-map or cluster diagram is easy. These diagrams consist of clusters or branches of related information radiating out from a central concept or idea. They usually look much like a spider's web or the top view of a tree when completed. To create one of these diagrams you will need:

- A fresh sheet of paper, at least 8.5-by-11 inches, though larger is generally better, especially for students who have large handwriting

- A flat surface to spread out on

- A pen or pencil — optionally, colored pens or markers can be used by students who enjoy color coding or have an artistic flare

To begin working on the diagram, place the broad topic of the research paper you are working on in a circle or box at the center of the page. If you do not have a broad topic, use the first thing that comes to mind. If you have a specific idea already, then use that. Add circles around your central idea containing other related thoughts that come to mind. Connect these circles back to the central topic with lines. Each of these ideas will become a branch in the diagram. Branches can be anything, even ideas you are not interested in including in your paper.

13 **Do not omit branches from your map.**
It can be tempting to censor your thought map, but write down everything that comes to mind. You never know what will end up connecting as the map progresses. Exercises such as mind-mapping work best when you just let the ideas flow and connect without placing restrictions on yourself or the map.

Inter-related concepts to branch from general concept

Once a branch is started, continue to work on related concepts to that branch as they come to mind, making the branch longer. Branches can split off into multiple sub-branches where needed. Whenever the ideas start coming slower, return to the main concept and begin a new branch. At any point, you can jump between branches to add things as they come to mind, but the goal is to get as many branches and as much information to work with as possible. If you are working with colored pens or markers, you can use a different color for ideas that stand out as useful or interesting to you as you go. Doodles can be included as part of these maps as well if they help organize the information or make it easier to remember.

14 **Get out the coloring supplies and have fun!**
Mind-mapping is especially effective for people who are visually oriented, but it can work for everyone. Because it is such a visual prewriting method, feel free to doodle and use an array of colors if it helps you sort through ideas. The more fun you have while making your map, the more relaxed you will be and the better your ideas will be.

Once you have several branches and many ideas pertaining to your topic, it is generally a good idea to pull back and look at the diagram as a whole.

You might notice some overlap in concepts and topics covered in each individual branch. If it does not make the diagram too cluttered, draw connecting lines between areas of the diagram that could be connected in the paper. You might wish to do the same with points of comparison or contrast, depending on what direction the research paper is going in. If the diagram is already cluttered, it is sometimes necessary to copy it over more neatly onto another sheet of paper or just make notations to yourself for later in some of the blank space left on the page.

If you were using the diagram to narrow down from a broad topic, pick out the particular branch or branches that seem like the best choice to write the paper on. You might then wish to do another web using this new, narrower topic, as the center of the map in order to generate specific ideas to research. If you started with a narrower topic, just pick out the branches that seem like the best choices to include in your paper.

Tech Savvy Option:

If you either do not have the room to make a pen and paper mind-map or you prefer a digital option, there are other options. Programs and websites for mind-mapping are becoming more common. Free Mind (**http://freemind.sourceforge.net**) is an open source program that allows you to make a mind-map on your computer to save and edit as you please. Best of all? It's free.

The following is a sample mind-map.

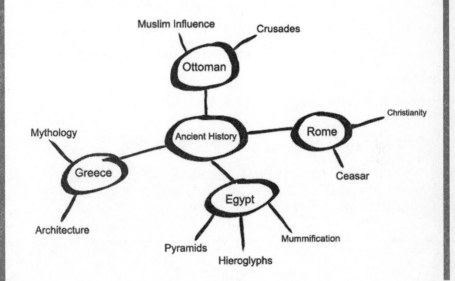

15 **Once the map is complete, go back and prune.**
After you have had time to look the map over and make notations, go back and choose the best ideas and bits of information to come out of the mapping session. Be discriminant and only choose the best ideas. If you do not like any of your ideas, you can always try again.

Freewriting

Freewriting is mind-mapping's less visually oriented cousin. Like mind-mapping, freewriting relies heavily on getting ideas down on paper as they come to you, placing quantity over quality for the time being. Unlike mind-mapping, these ideas are not laid out visually. Instead, they are just written down as they come to mind in one large block. The goal of freewriting is to force yourself to write a deluge of words that will later be edited and organized into a structured and coherent paper topic.

Freewrites can be handwritten or typed. Handwritten freewrites are much more common, but if being able to read your own quickly scribbled handwriting is a concern, typing might be a better choice. Freewriting does not have to be a timed activity, but when beginning, setting a timer for three to five minutes is usually a good idea, just to develop the habit.

> **Tip No.** **16** Set time goals when you first begin freewriting.
> If you have issues forcing yourself to prewrite or are unsure how long to prewrite, try using an egg timer or setting an alarm on your cell phone for three to five minutes, and then write until it goes off.

First thoughts that come to mind

Start by writing the general topic at the top of the paper as a jumping-off point, and then begin by writing the first thoughts that come to mind. The goal of the freewrite should be to keep the words flowing for the entirety of the activity, even if that means just writing the same word or phrase repeatedly until something else comes to mind. Tangents and unrelated thoughts are fine, though attempt to get back to the main ideas as soon as possible. When unsure of what to write, it is fine to write, "I don't know  what to write," or whatever else comes to mind when you think of your assignment. Again, the goal is quantity more than quality at this stage in the writing process.

No consideration or restraints on grammar and mechanics

It is important not place too much emphasis on proper spelling, grammar, or mechanics while freewriting. Punctuation is not necessary. Try to refrain from getting hung up on words you cannot spell or how to phrase ideas. Just keep writing ideas as they come to mind, regardless of how you feel about them, and eventually, you will find yourself writing down things that seem useful or interesting.

After the freewrite is completed, feel free to return to it with a critical eye. Underline or highlight any ideas that could turn into a topic for the paper or are specific points you know you will want to cover in the paper. As you pull these ideas out of the freewrite, make notations to yourself about any additional ideas that come to mind. All of these ideas will eventually be reworked into an outline and thesis statement. The more you start with, the less work you will have later. Ideas can also be tossed out later in the research process if they turn out to be unhelpful or there is a lack of information on the topic.

The following is a sample freewrite.

Ancient History Paper

Man, I really don't know what to write. I don't know what to do this paper about...it seems really long and hard and I don't really like ancient history that much...ancient history ancient history ancient history I saw a thing about greek mythology on TV the other day but it didn't really interest me so I don't really want to write about that though tomorrow there is supposed to be a show on about Egypt... When I was a kid I use to really like egypt and I had lots of books about mummies. Everyone does stuff about mummies though so maybe there is something else about egypt I can do. Pyramids sphinx giza nile crocodile hieroglyphs are neat.

```
Maybe I should look into the rosetta stone
and how hieroglyphs developed and how they
were eventually translated.
```

Why this method is effective

Freewriting is effective because it forces you to actually make notations of all of your passing thoughts on a topic. Many students get stuck while trying to determine what to write about because they feel like every idea they write down has to be good. The critical and logical part of the brain stifles the creative process. By temporarily turning off that critical process, ideas can flow freely without restriction. Sometimes, even unrelated thoughts can lead to great topics for papers — or at least ideas to look into relating to a particular topic. Freewrites are particularly helpful for students who tend to have many ideas for a paper and then forget them or dismiss them as bad as soon as it comes time to actually make an outline or write the paper.

Brainstorming and Listing

Most students are familiar with the concept of brainstorming. If you have ever sat around with your friends and tossed around ideas for what to do on a day off or where to go for lunch, you have brainstormed.

Brainstorming is often done in groups, classes, or committees to come up with ideas for fundraisers or parties, among other undertakings. Brainstorming is a great way to generate ideas and solve problems outside of a group setting, as well. Brainstorming for a paper works much like it does in a group setting, but in this case, you list ideas that come to mind by yourself.

Visual listing: Venn Diagrams

If you are a list person who also likes visual organization, consider using a Venn diagram.

To make a Venn Diagram, draw a circle on a sheet of paper and mark it with an idea. Draw additional, overlapping circles for other ideas. Once you have all of your main ideas listed, start listing sub-ideas inside of the appropriate circles. If an idea relates to more than one of the ideas, write it where those circles overlap. This is a great way to make a list and see how the ideas you have connect with each other.

Randomly generating ideas

Brainstorming is similar to freewriting in many ways. Ideas are generated randomly as they come to mind but are usually a bit more structured and organized than with freewriting. Unlike a mind-map, brainstorming does not necessarily flow neatly from one related concept to another. This method of generating ideas is more structured than freewriting and less visual than mind-mapping, so analytical students who enjoy having neat lists might find themselves gravitating toward this prewriting method. Brainstorming aims to create a large list of potentially useful information by forcing you to write down topic ideas or ideas to include in a paper, no matter how ridiculous or impossible they might seem.

Tip No. 17 If you are a "list maker," try brainstorming as a prewriting technique.

A huge part of successful prewriting is finding a style that works for you. People who are more analytical or list minded might have issues with the lack of formal structure in freewriting and mind-mapping, but making lists usually comes naturally.

Listing any ideas that come to mind on the topic

When brainstorming, you can use either a piece of paper or a word processor, whichever is more comfortable. Start by listing any ideas that come to mind. Try not to limit these ideas to ones that are realistic or helpful. Because this type of brainstorming is done alone, there is no need to worry about whether any ideas that come to mind are good; just write each topic or idea as it comes to you. Even if an idea is too broad or seems ridiculous, it might lead to a more useful idea later. While making this list, it is helpful to leave some space between each idea you write down so you can return to it and add any additional thoughts that come to mind as you go along. This should not turn into an outline, but for students who like to keep their lists neat and organized, having related sub-points on this list might be helpful. Additionally, once you do hit on an idea that works, you can start a new brainstorm of additional ideas to research or include in your paper.

The following is a sample brainstorming list.

```
Ancient History Paper
```

- Greek mythology
  - Athena
  - Math and architecture

- Egyptian history
  - Mummies and burial practices
  - Pyramids and architecture
  - Hieroglyphs

- Ottoman empire

- Roman invasion
  - Christianity and religion's part

Why These Techniques Work

The one thing each of these techniques has in common is the lack of emphasis on high quality and mechanics that will become more important later in the writing process. Even more structured methods, such as mind-mapping or brainstorming, allow students to write down ideas without second guessing themselves or feeling intimidated by formal structure. By feeling free to write about anything — even how annoying research papers are — ideas will flow naturally from one to the next. Rather than allowing these passing thoughts to become distractions, they can be written down, which allows the mind to move past them and onto the next thought. This greases the mental wheels, and eventually, topical ideas will start to flow and you will end up with at least one, if not multiple, useable topics.

Tip No. 18 Relax! Do not stress out over prewriting.
The more relaxed you are when you prewrite, the better material you will end up with. Focusing on high quality and perfectionism at this stage in the process creates undo stress that will just make picking a great topic and getting the paper underway more difficult.

Anything goes at this stage of the game, so have fun with it, and find what works for you. Try all of these methods, and see how they work, or even make up your own. As long as it gets your thoughts down on paper and helps generate some great ideas, it is a successful prewrite. Just remember to relax and ignore the part of the brain that wants to edit and make everything perfect right away. There will be plenty of time for that once you find the perfect topic.

Study Guide

❏ Prewriting should be done to help generate ideas for a paper. It is a vital step that will save you time later.

❏ Prewriting is a great way to narrow a broad assignment down into a handful of topics that actually interest you.

❏ Three common types of prewriting are Mind-mapping or Clustering, Freewriting, and Brainstorming or Listing.

   ❏ Mind-mapping involves constructing a web of interconnected ideas as they come to mind.

   ❏ Freewriting involves forcing yourself to write and write without stopping until you have generated ideas for your paper.

   ❏ Brainstorming is great for people who like lists because it allows you to list out any ideas that come to mind for your paper, regardless of how feasible they actually are.

❏ Prewriting methods can be combined or even invented, so if none of the methods discussed here are working, feel free to find what does work.

❏ Prewriting should be loose and less structured than normal writing, so relax, and do what comes naturally.

CASE STUDY: IMPORTANCE OF PREWRITING

Deanna Love
Writing Fellow (Carthage)
Information Literacy
Coordinator (St. Paul)
Carthage College Writing Center
St. Paul Public Library

I have worked at the Carthage College Writing Center for the past three years. Students using the Center include freshmen in their first seminar classes and seniors working on theses in a wide range of disciplines. The Center also serves students in the Adult Education program and the Target Language Experts, students from a variety of countries who come to Carthage to earn a Master's of Education while teaching introductory level language classes. During my time at the Center, I earned a level 3 Master tutor certification from the College Reading and Language Association. This certification requires a minimum of 30 hours of advanced training and 75 hours of face-to-face tutoring. I am currently working directly with the Writing Center Director to formulate a tutor training program designed to address the developmental writing needs of a portion of the student body requiring remedial writing help. I will soon begin a 12-month appointment with the Rondolo Community Outreach Library in St. Paul, Minnesota, as an Information Literacy Coordinator, supervising the Homework Help Center and providing tutor training emphasizing English Language Learner writing needs.

One of the biggest pieces of advice I can give is do not disregard the pre-writing stage. Time spent preparing to write saves time later. It also makes the entire paper-writing process less intimidating. It is much easier to consider writing a draft when you have concept maps, outlines, research notes, and a clear thesis statement. Be aware of how you use time, and try to determine the best way to divide up your homework hours. If you are struggling with time management, consider visiting a learning specialist to better understand your learning style. This knowledge can help you assess the areas in your homework or writing process that might need to be modified.

Focus and organization are two key factors that help to create strong papers. Students who are able to develop a specific thesis statement and then articulate the argument they propose in an organized manner tend to be much stronger writers than those who are unable to clearly state their ideas. Take your time, and do not be discouraged. Writing is a skill like any other and requires practice. Seek advice from experienced students, writing tutors, and your teachers. These resources can help you identify topics, form a thesis statement, and outline an argument.

Read the assignment. Read the assignment. Read the assignment. Often, teachers will provide clues for the type, tone, and topic of a paper directly within the assignment sheet. Look for key words and concepts. Then, use those key words to begin brainstorming possible ideas. Use concept maps or Venn diagrams to start organizing those initial thoughts. Review class notes and texts. Try freewriting — take five to ten minutes to just jot down any ideas/thoughts that come to you, without worrying about grammar, organization, or anything but what comes to the forefront of your mind. Take your time developing a strong, clear, and focused thesis statement. Perform any required research. Then, begin drafting your paper. When students invest more time in the pre-writing process, they face fewer struggles actually writing a paper.

Do not be afraid to ask the librarian for assistance — they will be delighted to help. Look at the sources referenced in the initial sources you find; often, those references can lead you to the key documents that play a foundational role in your topic. The Internet can be a powerful research tool, but always be aware of the possible weaknesses of an Internet source. Look for articles/sites provided by educational institutions or legitimate organizations. Ask your teacher if you have any doubts.

If you can force yourself to stay organized while prewriting, you will find it easier to organize your information later when you need to do your citations. It is absolutely essential to cite any idea that comes from another source. Please, please, please take the time to formulate citations when you initially find the information, and insert that citation into your paper immediately after using a source. Students lose so much time trying to go back at the end and remember each and every citation. Plagiarism can have drastic consequences in an academic setting, from failing the assignment, to failing the class, and even suspension or expulsion. Plagiarism is no joke, and it is imperative that every student learn how to cite sources. If you don't know how to cite sources, seek help. Your teacher, writing tutor, or librarian will be more than glad to teach you.

CHAPTER 4:

Narrowing Your Focus and Developing a Thesis Statement

Often, the biggest mistake students make when getting ready to write a research paper is choosing too broad of a topic. Although all of ancient Egyptian history might be interesting, trying to condense everything there is to say about it into a short research paper is a daunting, if not impossible, task. Jumping into the paper without narrowing the focus likely will leave you frustrated and confused later as you try to pick though all of the information you have and decide what to include. With a limited focus already in mind, however, choosing what information to include becomes a much less worrisome and time-consuming process. The trick is knowing when you have found the right topic.

Tip No. 19 **Start broad, and then whittle the topic down until it feels right.**

Prewriting forces you to generate many ideas, and the ideas you get from it will likely be too big to cover properly in your research paper. Recognizing this will allow you to zoom in on the most interesting or pertinent aspects of the topic that will make for the best paper.

Finding a Broad Focus, and Narrowing it Down

Recognizing a good paper topic when you come up with one can be easier said than done. Ideally, a good paper topic should be all of the following:

- Appropriate for the scope and subject matter of the class the paper is being written for

- Something you find interesting and will enjoy researching and writing about

- Easy to find good research materials for

- Have an argumentative aspect to it

- Not so broad that covering it would be impossible within the length of the paper

- Not so narrow that there is not enough to say on the subject

Understanding what a topic should cover and actually determining how to make the idea work as a viable research paper can be difficult. Sometimes, you will get lucky and hit on a topic that will require almost no additional refocusing, but far more often, you will need to tweak your idea slightly until it has a properly narrowed focus.

Tip No. **20** Understand that few topics will be perfect.

In an ideal world, any topic you choose would be exactly the right size and have tons of available resources, but this will not always be the case. Do not give up or get discouraged if something about your topic is giving you trouble or you find out later that it is a little too broad or narrow. These are fixable issues, so there is no need to panic.

How to narrow the focus

Students who have really taken to some of the prewriting techniques discussed in the previous chapter might find those same methods useful in narrowing the focus of their topic. If narrowing exactly what to focus on seems tough, try doing a mind-map or brainstorm some angles to approach the topic from. Another approach is to conduct some online searches for the topic to see what other people have said about it. Perusing the library's selection of books on your topic might give you an idea for how to approach the subject, as well. Most school libraries have access to not only books, but also electronic databases full of articles on almost every topic. Reading a few articles on a subject can be a great way to get ideas. Check the assignment parameters on the class syllabus or with the teacher to get some clues for how to narrow the focus as well. Even bouncing ideas off friends and classmates can be useful. Most importantly, make sure to take full advantage of all of the resources available to you. Many schools have more resources for writing papers than students expect, so ask a librarian or teacher for some help if you are unsure of what you have at your disposal.

Litmus Test

Consider these questions a sort of "litmus test" for your paper. A litmus test is used in chemistry to test the pH of a substance, but the term is also used in other situations and is often applied to some sort of crucial pass-fail test. Your topic does not have to pass this test with a score of 100 percent, but the better it fairs when you ask yourself these questions, the easier things will be for you later. Often, there will be at least one category where you cannot help it if your topic "fails." You might be required to write a paper on a classic piece of literature, such as *Hamlet*, that has been written about by hundreds, if not thousands, of scholars. You might have to write an argumentative research paper on a hot-button issue for a politics class. If it is part of the assignment, that is fine, but try to make the paper as strong as possible in every area where you can help it. You will save yourself a headache later.

Asking yourself questions will help narrow the focus or make sure you have narrowed your focus properly. Once you have an idea or two for how you might want to tighten up your research topic, try using the following checklist to determine whether you are on the right track:

1. **Is this topic still too broad?** Sometimes, you might think you have narrowed your topic down enough, but you might still be too broad for the time and length of the project. A good way to test this is to do an online search for your refined topic and see what sort of information pops up. If professionals have written volumes about your topic, it might be too broad for a five-page research paper (though you might want to save it for a final project, or even

a college research paper, later). For now, try picking one element of your topic to really focus on, and see if that helps.

2. **Is this topic too narrow?** On the other side of the first question, sometimes in the effort to get away from being too broad, students go too far in the other direction and wind up with topics too narrow for the scope of their papers. If you have to write a long research paper and can only find a handful of research materials that touch on your subject, you might need to expand slightly. Try finding a related aspect of the same topic to include in your argument or another way to expand the focus slightly. If all else fails, refocus and save the too-narrow topic for a short paper later.

3. **Does this topic fit the parameters of the assignment?** Between prewriting, preliminary research, getting the topic narrowed, and everything else, students sometimes lose sight of what the original assignment was. Before you commit to a topic, double-check the assignment information, and make sure your topic meets all the requirements given to you by your teacher. If it does not, determine whether there is a way to adjust it slightly to get all of the requirements in. Bounce ideas off classmates, or meet with your teacher to discuss how to make the topic work if you find yourself stuck.

4. **Is this topic argumentative?** With rare exceptions, every research paper should be argumentative in some way. Research papers are not just about compiling a bunch of research and then repeating everything you discovered about a topic. The best papers aim to convince the reader of something based on the research that has been gathered. For example, a paper might argue that Paul Revere was given too much credit for his part in the Revolutionary War or

that noneducational TV programming is often more accurate than educational programs. Try to find controversy within the topic, and craft an argument from that. If there is no way to make the topic argumentative, you might need to find a way to refocus it to find an argument.

5. **Is the topic too controversial?** Argumentative is good, but sometimes going with too controversial of a topic can be too much to handle. Certain subjects are deemed taboo or get everyone riled up when they are mentioned. If you find that your topic is embroiled in too much controversy, you might need to pick and choose what you want to cover. Controversial topics can make some of the best research papers, but they need to be treated delicately. Students who are intimidated by arguments or being challenged about their opinions might want to stick to safer topics.

6. **Why is this important?** (Also known as "Who cares?") This question absolutely needs an answer. If the answer to "Who cares?" is "No one" or "I don't know," you might need to find a new topic or, at the least, refocus it. If the writer does not know why anyone would want to read a research paper on his or her topic, then odds are good that the readers will not know why the writer bothered to write it. Determine whom this topic will appeal to and then keep that audience in mind while writing the paper.

7. **Are there enough materials available for me to research this?** Always do a preliminary check for research materials before committing to a topic. Few things are more frustrating than finding what seems to be a great topic and then, after doing all of the preliminary work, finding out there are not enough reliable sources on the topic to do a proper paper. Checking the library

and electronic databases is a good place to start. Generally, when working on an average-length paper, if you cannot find sources that look credible while doing a quick search, you might want to adjust your focus to find more sources. It is possible to do a paper without many readily available sources; it just makes the process more challenging.

8. **Is this topic fresh?** Is there still something to say about it? Be particularly wary of this one if the topic you have chosen turns up a ton of sources. Having lots of research materials available is nice and makes things easier, but if a topic has been around for a while or is a hot-button issue, then finding something new and creative to say about it might be difficult. Topics such as Shakespeare's *Hamlet*, gun control, and the death penalty are good examples. These topics have tons of information out there, but scholars and pundits have written so much about them that it can be hard to find something new or innovative to say. If you are set on writing your paper on a topic like this, find out if there is anything fresh being written about it by looking for recently dated articles. Also, be extra careful when wording your thesis statement to make sure you are not making the same points as everyone else.

If the topic passes this checklist, with or without some adjustments along the way, then odds are good it is the start of a great paper. It might need to undergo later revision, but for now, you are ready to start working on developing this topic into your paper's thesis statement.

Tip No. 21 Have a backup – just in case.
Even if you think your topic is absolutely perfect, it does not hurt to have a backup idea in mind, just in case you run into unforeseen trouble later and have to change. Keep a couple variations on your narrowed-down topic on file somewhere. Even if they do not come in handy for this paper, they might come in handy for another one later.

Developing a Thesis Statement

The term "thesis statement" has been thrown around quite a bit in this book already. It is obviously an important part of writing a research paper, but the difference between a refined topic and a thesis statement might be a bit unclear. In short, the topic of a paper is what the paper hopes to cover or prove in a loosely defined sense. A thesis statement, by comparison, is a declarative statement made in the introduction of the paper that lets the reader know what the paper is going to inform them about. More than that, the thesis statement should serve as the framework for writing your paper, from start to finish. The thesis statement is one of the most vital aspects of the paper because it is not only a guide for the writer, but it should also grab the readers and convince them that this paper is worth taking the time to read. A weak thesis statement is often the sign of a weak paper, and the last thing students want is for their teachers to label their writing as weak from the beginning. Even if the rest of the paper is well-written, having a weak thesis will make the paper feel unfocused or lacking.

Tip No.

22 The thesis statement is the framework, or guide, for your paper, so make sure it is as strong as possible.

For the rest of the writing process, you will be referring back to the thesis statement. It will help you write your outline, and all of your research will be done in order to support this thesis statement. It is the most important sentence of any paper, so give it the time and effort it deserves.

Creating the frame: Turning a topic into a thesis

By now, you should have some notations about your chosen topic and what you are thinking of covering within it. You might even have some backup ideas in case your focus changes during the research process. Turning that information into a solid thesis is fairly simple but can often be difficult, as well. The process itself is not difficult, but as with any skill, it requires practice and can take several tries to get it right. Thesis statements are often intimidating to writers, but remember that they can always be revised (and will likely need to be revised slightly as you do more research), so do not let yourself get too stressed out about it at this stage. However, be sure to take the time to craft the best thesis statement you can now because it will save time and frustration throughout the process.

When beginning to craft a thesis, there are a few things writers should keep in mind. A solid thesis statement should meet all of the following criteria:

- It is a statement of the paper's overall message and purpose.

- It must be declarative.

- It has a clear direction or frame for the paper.

- It needs to have a hook to make it interesting.

- It must be clearly worded and concise.

- It must be void of weak language.

These points make a great checklist to keep handy while crafting a thesis. The following section will take a more in-depth look at each of them.

For Science Students

The thesis statement is a lot like your paper's hypothesis. It is what you hope to prove with your paper, much like a hypothesis is what you believe you will prove with an experiment. The difference is that you do not know if you will prove your hypothesis at the start of an experiment, whereas your entire paper should be structured to support and prove your thesis. Structurally, there will be some differences, but if you can write a hypothesis, you can write a thesis statement. If you are writing about your own scientific research, your hypothesis can even be edited to become your paper's thesis statement.

Paper's overall message and purpose

The thesis statement describes the point of your paper to readers. A good place to start when drafting a thesis is to ask yourself "What point am I trying to make in this paper?" This relates to the argumentative aspect. Based on the little preliminary research you have done and what you already know about your topic, you should have an idea of what you are hoping to prove. It might be something such as, "I will prove gun control laws should be more/less restrictive," or "I will show that Paul Revere did not have as large of a role in the American Revolution as people think." Although statements such as these are not great thesis statements (and might not be considered thesis statements at all), with a little work, they can turn into great thesis statements. If this step is proving to be difficult, try doing a bit more research or asking yourself questions until you form a solid opinion on your topic. You might change this opinion later, but have an idea going into your paper of where it will end up and what conclusions you will draw.

Declarative statement

Once you have nailed down your paper's central point or purpose, the next step is to make sure what you are saying about the subject is a focused declarative statement. Do not meander away from your point. State whatever you are hoping to prove with authority. This is an opinion on the topic, but by doing the research necessary to write this paper, you are becoming an authority on the topic. Act like one! Avoid using words that make it seem as though you are questioning your knowledge or authority on the subject. Phrases such as "I think" or "I feel" weaken your argument. Instead, use statements such as "This paper will... ." Anyone reading your paper assumes that what you are arguing is your own opinion and that whatever is stated in the paper is what the paper is hoping to prove. Restating this information adds extra bulk to your thesis and does not look professional. You want to be streamlined and authoritative if you want to get noticed.

Also, never use a question as part of your thesis statement. Including questions might seem like an interesting stylistic choice or way to draw in readers. Sometimes, this can be used effectively, but far more often, it makes writers seem either unsure of what they are trying to prove or as if they are asking the readers for their opinion. This paper should showcase your knowledge and the research you have done. By using a question, you take the spotlight off yourself. Stating the point of the paper — and stating it with absolute authority — is key in writing a thesis statement that will impress teachers.

Picking a direction

Now that you have a clear sense of the purpose of your paper and you are sure your phrasing carries authority, it is time to give your statement more direction. Get out the notes you have taken so far, and pick a few things you know you want to include in your paper. These ideas should help form the basis for your thesis statement, so be sure to pick supporting ideas that underscore the main point and add credibility to your argument. You can always change these later, but the thesis statement should act as a frame for your paper. This means it should include information about which key points will be covered in the paper to support the main argument.

For example, a paper on enacting more restrictive gun regulations might prove it has a direction with a thesis statement such as: "Gun control regulations might restrict the purchase of certain weapons, but they do not do enough to keep guns out of the hands of dangerous criminals or ensure citizens who purchase guns know how to properly use them." The reader knows the paper will be arguing that gun control regulations should be stricter. He or she also knows the author will be arguing that more needs to be done to keep guns out of the hands of certain people and that people who purchase guns should receive more training on how to properly use them. Not only does this give the reader clues as to what to expect in the paper, but it also gives the author a reference point to return to while writing the paper. If you get lost while writing your paper and are unsure of what to write next or where to include a piece of information, the thesis statement should serve as a road map that will answer these questions and as the basis for writing an outline. *Writing an outline will be covered in Chapter 6.*

Tip No.

23 Remember, you can always change your thesis statement later.

If it helps reduce the pressure, think of the thesis statement you are crafting now as a temporary thesis statement. It is a placeholder for the thesis statement that will end up in your final paper. Later on, once you have done more research, you can always revise your thesis if the direction of the paper has changed. In a perfect world, students would never have to revise their thesis statements, but opinions can change as they become more informed, and sometimes, students will even disprove their original thesis through research.

Craft a hook

Once you have a thesis statement that states the main point of the paper and outlines the direction in which the argument is headed, the bulk of the work is complete. These elements are the meat of a thesis statement. The rest of the work is adding the depth and finesse that get a paper noticed. Make sure the thesis statement has a hook to ensure your paper has "punch" or "pizzazz." If the thesis statement is boring, readers will not be interested in taking the time to read the rest of the paper. Starting off with a fact or piece of information that is shocking or otherwise attention grabbing is a great way to achieve this. For example, rather than simply stating that divorces are bad for children, you might say "When compared to children who have suffered a death in the family, children from divorced homes experience more psychological trauma and mental health issues later in life, which is why society needs to reexamine relationship and familial expectations." This statistic is surprising, and it grabs the reader's attention, which encourages him or her to continue reading. Topics that are already controversial or widely appealing usually already have the intensity and interest without a lot of extra effort, but some topics might require a bit more time to add flair. Regardless of the topic, the thesis statement should have style and be written in your own voice.

Often, adding style to writing is something that students find difficult, especially because writing with a unique voice is something that is difficult to teach. It takes time and practice to develop a writing style. Just remember that the topic you have chosen to write about is something interesting to you. Think about why you find the topic interesting, and make sure the thesis statement reflects that. Let your personality show in your writing. Reading other papers and essays will give you an idea of what makes a unique style, but in the end, just be genuine, and your style will show through in your words.

Tip No.

24 Be yourself.

It can be tempting to try to sound lofty and academic in papers, but writing in your own style will help make a paper stand out from the pile. Developing style is a hard thing to teach, but it comes with practice. Keep in mind the level of formality required for a research project. Writing in "your own style" is not an excuse for poor writing, sloppy wording, or inappropriate language. Your style will come out in the descriptions you give and the examples you use. Once you have the mechanics down and you are not worried about slipping into a tone that is too informal, you can write what comes naturally. When you are relaxed and trying to have fun with a project, it shows and naturally makes the topic more interesting to readers.

Be clear and concise

Like writing with style, writing concisely takes practice. Students often make the mistake of being exorbitantly verbose, or overly wordy, in their writing. It can be tempting to whip out the thesaurus whenever you get stuck and find a big word to add flair or use too many words to state simple ideas. Many students suffer from the misconception that more or bigger words somehow make their writing better or sound smarter. Usually, these extra or complicated words just muddy the waters and make it difficult to understand the point the author is trying to make. This is not to say that students should not use their vocabularies to their advantage, but rather, they should make sure they use these words to maximum effect. In the thesis statement, especially, never use two words when one will do, and try to keep the wording straightforward. A good way to ensure you are doing this is to go through your thesis statement and cross out every word that is not directly contributing to the main idea of the sentence. Add back in any words that are absolutely necessary so the sentence still makes grammatical sense. Usually this will reveal places where some excess fat can be trimmed from your wording. Remember, you need to condense the point of your paper into one to two sentences, so use what little space you have as wisely as possible.

Pruning a Sentence

This is a writing exercise that many writing classes employ to teach students how to write concisely. It is a form of extreme editing, and it is a great tool to help you understand what the most important parts of a sentence are. To practice pruning a sentence, you will need to take a sentence, in this case your thesis statement, that is not as concise as you would like it. Here is a sample thesis statement from a paper about Edgar Allan Poe's "The Tell-Tale Heart." In order to prune it down, all the nonessential parts of the sentence have been crossed out.

> ~~Though the~~ narrator assures ~~the~~ reader
> ~~several times that he is~~ not mad
> ~~it seems as though he is~~ trying ~~to~~
> convince himself ~~of this fact, rather~~
> ~~than the reader, as these instances~~
> ~~only work to further~~ illuminate
> ~~his~~ insanity.

This entire statement was pruned down to ten important words. See how much fluff there was? Now that the excess has been trimmed, go back in and add words that are needed to make it a complete sentence again.

> The narrator assures the reader repeatedly he is not mad, but he is actually trying to convince himself of this, as each instance further illuminates his insanity.

See how much shorter and more concise this sentence is? It gets the same information across in half the space.

Choosing the right words

Mark Twain once said, "The difference between the right word and the almost right word is like the difference between lightning and a lightning bug." The goal is to write a thesis statement that will impress, so it is vital to choose strong words. After all, which is more impressive: lightning or a lightning bug? The answer is obvious, so use strong words as much as possible. Chances are good that while trimming excess words from your thesis statement, you removed a lot of weak words. Always be sure to double-check for repeated words and poor word choices before finalizing a thesis statement. Qualifying words and phrases, such as "sort of," "kind of," "a bit," "really," and "very" add extra fluff without telling the reader anything useful. When qualifiers are needed to describe something, try to use more quantitative phrasing when possible. For example, you might say, "60 percent of" instead of "most of." The word "that" is also overused. Many sentences that use the word "that" can be reworded so that "that" is not included. For example, the previous sentence could read, "Many sentences can be reworded to remove the word 'that' from them entirely," which reads much more clearly.

> **Tip No. 25 Make yourself sound credible.**
> We will discuss credibility more in the next chapter, but avoid using dodgy words or vague language in your thesis. Such tricks are often used to cover up the fact that writers do not have all the facts to back up what they are saying. You will have all the facts, and you should have nothing to hide, so write a paper that sounds like it. If you question your own credibility, other people will, too

When choosing powerful words, be aware of clichés. It can be tempting to use cute or clichéd language to try to spice up a paper or give it more personal flair. By nature, these statements are overused and lack creativity. If, for some reason, using clichéd language is unavoidable, try to put a new or creative spin on it. Still, this can make a paper seem unprofessional or cheesy, so use this approach with caution. It may be true that clichés can occasionally be used effectively, but teachers might still frown upon their use, so it is best to avoid them as much as possible. By that same token, avoid slang and informal phrasing unless it relates directly to the topic. The thesis statement, as well as the rest of the paper, should be as polished and professional as possible, so do not use language and phrasing inappropriate to an academic or professional setting.

Simple versus Complex Thesis Statements

Most papers will only require a simple thesis statement. When you first start writing research papers, simple thesis statements will be enough of a challenge. There may be times, however, when a complex statement is needed to properly convey the paper's purpose. A paper for an advanced composition class, or a final project in an AP course, are examples of times when this might be the case. The simplest thesis statements follow some variation on a basic "This is true because of these reasons," or "Despite this opposing viewpoint, these reasons are why this is true" formula. More complex topics might require longer thesis statements that come in two parts, where the first sentence sets up the argument and then the second sentence gives the real point of the paper and the supporting reasons. Use whatever is appropriate to the situation.

Thesis Statement Examples

By now, you should have a solid understanding of what makes or breaks a thesis statement. Below, you will find nine sample thesis statements, each with a few issues that need to be resolved. These issues are then explained, and a revised alternate example is listed for your reference.

1. **Shakespeare's *Romeo and Juliet* is odd for a tragedy.**

   This is an OK start for a thesis statement, but it lacks specifics. Why is it odd? Where is the argument going? Although these questions might not be answered entirely in the thesis statement, they should at least be addressed.

Revised: With the exception of the opening lines, the beginning of *Romeo and Juliet* is set up using the comedic conventions of Elizabethan theater, which makes it Shakespeare's strangest tragedy.

2. **Sharks do not kill as many people as people seem to think they do, so the media-portrayed shark threat is overblown and stupid.**

This thesis statement is far too wordy. The word "people" is repeated unnecessarily, and language such as "overblown and stupid" lacks professionalism. There is also little specific language here to back up what this person is trying to say or give the paper a direction.

Revised: Sharks pose very little risk to humans and kill less than one person in the United States per year. Despite this, pop culture and media portrayals hype the danger unnecessarily.

3. **Current gun control laws do a lot to keep some types of weapons off the streets, but they do not do enough to keep guns away from criminals or teach consumers how to use them.**

This thesis statement is not terrible, but it uses vague language in the beginning. It is a little wordier than necessary and a little flat, too. It lacks "oomph" or passion. Again, this thesis statement is not bad or wrong, but it is not an award winner, either.

Revised: Regulations on military-grade weapons and ammunition, for example, do help to keep dangerous weapons off the streets, but gun control regulations are still strongly lacking when it comes to keeping guns away from criminals and teaching civilians how to properly use the weapons they are able to purchase.

4. **Many of Egypt's historical artifacts are housed in London, not Cairo, like they should be.**

This sentence lacks a lot of punch. It also does not strongly present the paper's argument. It starts to give a direction, but fails to fully flesh that out. It also lacks a lot of finesse. It is still an OK starting point for a thesis statement, but it needs some "oomph" and a little more substance to make it sound stronger.

Revised: To this day, England's museums house more Egyptian artifacts than the Egyptian Museum, which is located in Cairo, despite attempts to rectify this. Although delicate artifacts could be destroyed or damaged by relocating them, several other pieces should be moved back to Cairo because they are part of the Egypt's rich history and many of them were obtained unethically.

5. **I believe that as long as news media remains a business, bias will remain in the media because reporters must report news that sells.**

The "I believe" in the statement automatically weakens this thesis statement. It does state the main point of the paper, but it is otherwise lackluster and weak. It needs a stronger direction, also, because it does not set up a strong frame for this paper. The reader is not sure what exactly will be covered, and the author might get lost while writing without that solid framework.

Revised: Ethically, journalists have a responsibility to report all news accurately and without bias, but the media is a business and must report news that makes money. Donations and affiliations with corporations that keep media companies afloat perpetuate bias and unethical reporting.

6. **Despite not being formally recognized by most literary scholars as part of the canon, J.R.R. Tolkien is one of the most influential authors of the last century.**

This is actually a good example. It states an argument, and the fact that Tolkien fantasy has had a resurgence in popularity recently adds an element of interest to it. It still could frame the argument a bit better, however.

Revised: J.R.R. Tolkien's works are timeless and inspiring, and they have contributed to the literary community, so they should be recognized by scholars as part of the literary canon.

7. **The portrayal of criminologists on television is bad for the criminal justice field because it floods the field with students and job seekers who don't really understand the profession.**

The language here is a bit informal. The use of a contraction is frowned upon, if not forbidden, in almost every academic setting. The rest of the thesis is not horrible, but the use of ambiguous words, such as "bad," does not give it the right authoritative tone.

Revised: Although the glamorous portrayal of criminal justice work in pop culture might increase the number of students studying this important field, it ultimately hurts the profession by flooding the job market with misinformed individuals who do their jobs incorrectly and do not enjoy the work.

8. **Despite the evolution of higher-resolution graphics and more lifelike controls in recent years, video game brutality does not consequentially impact the cognitive development or behavioral tendencies of today's progeny.**

   This is what happens when you try to add style and flair by going through a thesaurus and replacing words with bigger, "more intelligent" ones. Doing this sparingly to come up with more potent words is OK, but when overdone, it just makes your writing more difficult to understand. Also, starting with a word like "despite" makes it seem as though the author is hoping better graphics will negatively affect children, which is opposite of what is actually being argued.

   Revised: There is no significant evidence to prove that video game violence has a negative impact on a child's cognitive or behavioral development, even with the advent of higher-resolution graphics and more lifelike displays.

9. **Webcomics are totally increasing in popularity, gaining a lot of cred in the industry. They are starting to overtake print comics and might soon give them the boot entirely.**

   This example takes using informal language and slang to the extreme. Trying to add interest by using phrasing such as "cred" and "the boot" might work with your friends, but in a professional academic setting, it comes off as juvenile and will give most teachers the wrong impression. If this were a paper about the use of slang in modern culture, it might be more appropriate, but in this example, your thesis statement could be filled with words that would better define the direction of the paper and give it more substance.

Revised: Due to the popularity of the Internet, Webcomics are starting to overtake print comics in popularity and will play a key role in the future of the comic industry, despite critics dismissing them as a lower art form.

Tip No.

26 Make your point, and then say why.

The most vital components of a thesis statement are the "what" and the "why." Any thesis statement needs to explain what point the paper is making and then give a basic reason, or several reasons, why this argument is valid. As long as you remember to make a solid point and then use your support to give your paper direction, you will be well on your way to a great thesis statement. If there is one part of a thesis statement that you absolutely cannot get wrong, this is it.

CASE STUDY: THESIS STATEMENTS AND GREAT PAPERS

Maria Carrig
Associate Teacher of English and Theater
Carthage College

I have been a college teacher of English since 1994 (17 years). I have graded countless papers and taught the writing and editing of papers.

A great paper has several virtues. First, it shows an understanding that ideas matter, that anything worth writing about should matter not just to the writer but to the audience of the writer (fellow students, fellow writers, the world). It has a sense of drama. The writer might be trying to analyze a text, explore an issue, or prove a point. The great paper not only does this successfully, but also gives the reader an answer to the question "so what?" Second, a great paper, however creative and offbeat, shows a rational, logical mind at work. The reader can follow and be convinced by its movement from one idea to the next. Third, a great paper has that elusive quality called "voice": it shows originality of thought and expression, and careful, elegant, and creative choice of words.

And a fourth point: Think of your finished product like you think of going on a date: Appearances matter! You want your reader (your "date") to see that you have taken the time to make a good impression because you respect yourself and you respect him or her.

Spend an adequate amount of time working on your thesis statement. Ideally, a thesis statement answers a difficult or complex question or problem, one that matters to readers within the framework set up by the writer. Clarity is important, but don't oversimplify, or you may end up proving the obvious or arguing something absurd.

I had problems with writer's block and procrastination throughout my career as a student (still do). Overcoming these involves breaking the process into manageable parts: freewriting, keeping the words flowing even when ideas aren't coming; showing my work to others at every stage I can; and most importantly, creating the time to write and not allowing myself to be distracted when it is my writing time.

Although there are a lot of mechanical elements to writing well, becoming a writer is a lot less quantifiable than the mastering of rules. Good writers read a lot and, consciously or unconsciously, imitate the writers they like. Good writers write a lot, including informal private writing like journals, commonplace books (collections of quotes, ideas, fragments), poetry notebooks, etc. Good writers share their writing and know that writing is like a conversation — with friends, with other writers and texts, with oneself. It is never finished, and it is never perfect, but that is the beauty of it.

Study Guide

❏ Narrowing the focus properly is important. Make sure you consider the type and length of the paper you are writing before you begin narrowing the focus.

❏ Once you have an idea for a narrowed focus, run it through the checklist found in this chapter to make sure it passes.

❏ Consider keeping a backup topic or two in mind, just in case you run into problems later during the writing process and need to shift directions.

❏ Once you have a narrowed topic, the next step is to construct a thesis statement. This thesis statement is the most important sentence in the entire research paper, and it will be a road map for your research and planning.

❏ A good thesis statement should:

   ❏ Be a statement of the paper's overall message and purpose.
   ❏ Be declarative.
   ❏ Have a clear direction or frame for the paper.
   ❏ Have a hook to make it interesting.
   ❏ Be clearly worded and concise.
   ❏ Be void of weak language.

❏ Read your thesis statement over several times, or have friends or tutors check it for weak spots to be sure it is as strong as it can be.

❏ Remember that you are still early in the writing process and you can always change or alter your thesis to better fit the research you do later.

CHAPTER 5:

Research

Now that you have a
narrow topic and a good
idea where you want to go
with it, it is time to start

researching the topic. The research collected in this stage will provide the
backbone for your paper. Researching provides its own unique challenges,
however, and many students fall into common traps without even realizing
it. This chapter will help you avoid some of these common pitfalls, as well
as teach you how to find and evaluate sources of information.

CASE STUDY: RESEARCHING LIKE A PROFESSIONAL

Karl R. Olson
Curriculum Management Specialist
Herzing University

Undergraduate degrees in politics and government as well as in international relations gave me plenty of opportunity to work on my paper-writing skills. Before I was finished, I knew several different methods to present the information the instructor wanted, defend my opinion, or use a paper as an exploration of idea that allowed the writing of the paper to be a learning tool and not just an assessment of learning.

A graduate program in information systems management and a graduate certificate program in project management both required a very different style than I was used to. Paper writing had to contain a much more persuasive element. It was not enough to just tell what I thought and back it up with references that agreed or supported me. I had to truly sell my ideas by giving the what, why, how, where, and when and also include analysis of costs, risks and benefits. Papers had to be, or appear to be, evidence based.

My work experience has included teaching college-level courses, teaching graduate-level adjunct faculty, and developing curriculum with subject matter experts who may not have formal education training. Quite often I have used papers to assess aptitude prior to engaging in a training regime or project, and often I have used papers to assess learning during and at the end of training.

A great paper reminds me of how exciting it is to learn. Most people can pound out a paper and regurgitate the information in a text or lecture, and these are painful and repetitive to read. Many people can write an essay, to whatever length you assign, telling you how many ways their opinion is right and why you must agree with them. Reading these papers often feels like listening to a salesman sell something you would never buy. The best papers don't preach at you or fulfill requirements. All by themselves, they start a conversation with the reader, walking you through what it was like to be ignorant on a subject and how careful you had to be learning the information and picking, screening, and verifying sources. Really great papers walk you through the missteps of learning and accept mistakes as part of the learning process. In the end, they do not leave you feeling like someone was trying to tell you what you wanted to hear or that someone was trying to sell you on an idea, but they leave you feeling like you were having a rational conversation. In the end, you don't have to agree with a great paper to appreciate it; you simply know that a rational person would agree with the argument as presented, even if you, as the grader, do not.

Write humbly. Never use Wiki. Find sources your instructor did not recommend. Find someone to review it, and make the suggested changes before submitting the paper. Many modern students have never been taught how to research. Research is not a Google search. Many universities offer classes or assistance in how to research. Once enough research has been started, be prepared to plan. A research paper is not stream of consciousness, and you have to think about the order and flow of your presentation and arguments. Start early, and make enough time to complete the paper.

I always suggest taking one page of paper and writing down what the subject is, what the resources needed will be, and a brief basic idea of the order of the paper. Allow yourself to be flexible; the research you do might change your opinions or idea of what is most important as the paper progresses.

Start with peer-reviewed journals. Research the authors of relevant information. Check their cited sources and their past writings. Be aware of the date of publication of the information, and be aware that new research may have contradicted your original sources. Always look for the people who most credibly argue against your original sources. Their cited references will be a wealth of possibilities, and the argument against your original source will help you identify possible biases your source had.

The only change between now and when the Internet was not available is that information is easier to get and credibility takes more work to verify. The standards remain exactly the same. Peer-reviewed information is much more valuable than journals or blogs. The researcher must be very aware of who the intended audience of the information was, what the sources are, and if there was any bias or agenda involved in the publication of this material.

Find and use an organizational style that truly works for you, not just one you can claim works for you. Many people get frustrated or feel self-conscious that they do not have a traditional organizational style and never let themselves find the style that works best for them. You can organize by subject, date research published, alphabetical by author, or even by common references cited. The test is if you can follow and visually demonstrate an argument through your own organizational structure. Generally, if you can do it at your desk, you can do it in the paper.

A research paper is intimidating. Think of it in smaller pieces. Outline writing – initial research – revision – more research – rough draft – more research – more drafts – polishing – citation page – editing. Make sure you plan enough time for each stage; small stages are easier to manage time-wise.

Every bit of advice given here is advice I learned the hard way.

Finding Credible Sources

While working on a research paper, you will likely hear a lot about making sure your sources are "credible." On the surface, this sounds like an obvious and easy piece of advice to follow, but in practice, it can be much more difficult. A source's credibility is, in essence, how trustworthy its information is. Many writers tend to believe that all information in print is automatically true. In reality, it is easy for anyone to voice an opinion or present false information as fact without any credentials or proof of what they are saying, especially with the popularity of the Internet. Often, sources like these will appear credible, even when they are not, so students must be wary.

Tip No. 27 Be a skeptical researcher.
Just because something is presented as fact does not mean it is. Just because something is written in a book, article, or other type of source does not make it entirely accurate or even true. It can seem paranoid to research this way, but you will end up with higher-quality sources if you question everything and double-check your facts.

Examining source credentials and affiliations

Always research the background of any source you are considering using for your paper. Some sources will be obviously untrustworthy, but many will be presented as legitimate or seem to have credentials when they do not. The following are some points to consider when evaluating the credibility of a source:

- **What are the author's credentials?** Do not be fooled by fancy titles or degrees when reading an author's pedigree. Make sure the credentials they list are actually pertinent. Having a degree does not make someone an expert in every field, so be sure the author of any source is actually qualified to speak on it with authority, whether it be because they have personal experiences or academic qualifications.

- **What associations or affiliations does the author or publisher have?** If the author or publisher is associated with certain special interest groups or specific points of view, this can lead to bias. Authors or publishers who are associated with less than savory practices or activities might be less than credible, as well. If an author or publisher of a potential resource is associated with a specific bias, this does not automatically make it a bad source, but be aware of the slant of the information before using it.

- **Does the source have any noticeable bias?** How to specifically look for signs of bias will be discussed later in this chapter, but sometimes it can be quite obvious. Finding unbiased sources is usually for the best, but finding a truly unbiased source is nearly impossible in many cases. Heavily biased sources can be used effectively with some topics, but they should generally be avoided. Understanding the side an article is taking will allow you to question the information being presented and make sure it is factual and usable in your own research.

- **Does the author cite any sources? Are these sources credible?** Unless the author of the source was an eyewitness to an event or is analyzing data from personal experiments, his or her information has to come from somewhere. Beware of anonymous sources or authors who do not list where information comes from. This makes it hard to fact check any claims made in an article. When authors do list sources, always review them and make sure the sources stand up to scrutiny.

- **Is the source outdated?** Due to the rapid speed at which technology moves, information goes out of date quickly. With some topics, such as historical events, having information written a long time ago is not an issue and might even be helpful, as it was written when what you are writing about actually happened. In most cases, though, check the dates on any sources you are considering, and make sure they are not so old that they no longer are relevant or applicable.

- **Is the source incomplete or abridged?** Some sources might not seem to be biased until you realize they are missing information. They might have taken information out of context and used it to support an argument or edited it in other ways. Some sources might actually be excerpts from a larger source, as well. This can cause you to misunderstand what the source is about and use the information in it improperly or out of context.

- **What endorsements or reviews has the source gotten?** Book sources will often have reviews printed right on them, so check whether any reputable people have given it an endorsement. Online retailers of books will usually have reviews as well, so check to see what people are saying about sources. You can usually find reviews of larger reputable websites, as well. Some smaller sources, journal articles for example, might not have reviews readily available, but many times, reputable authors will have a large body of work, so find out whether the author has any endorsements or has written other things that were well reviewed.

- **Is the publisher of the source reputable?** Large publishers or reputable magazines and journals will usually fact check the information they are putting out pretty thoroughly, so using sources from well-known publishers is usually safe. Some publishers might have a reputation for printing anything, so fact checking falls to the consumer. On the flip-side, some publishers might have a reputation for printing false information, such as some tabloid papers for example, so use information from publishers with a negative reputation with caution.

- **Does the source use loaded or vague terms to support itself?** We discussed the importance of being specific when crafting a thesis statement. The same rule applies when choosing sources. Beware of sources that use vague terms, such as "recent studies show" or "many people believe," without giving any citations to back up these claims. Some sources also will use buzzwords to play on the emotions of readers. Both of these traits are red flags and should make you at the very least fact check the information being given. However, you might need to disregard it entirely.

- **Does the author or publisher of the source have an ulterior motive or agenda?** This partially relates to the second bullet in this list. Depending on who or what the author or publisher is affiliated with, this might color the information presented. If the author or publisher is pushing a product, for example, they likely have an ulterior motive and might slant the information being presented. Authors or publishers affiliated with political, governmental, or other special interest groups run into the same issue.

Evaluating for areas of bias

All sources that are not simply lists of data or statistics will be biased in some respects. Try as authors might to be fair and unbiased, partiality still creeps in. Because every person has a slightly different perspective

on life and events, that perspective will color the way an author presents information. In some cases, the bias is so minor it might be unnoticeable, but in others, it is the predominant message of the text and prevents the author from presenting information accurately. Just because a source is biased does not mean it is unusable. Sometimes, biased sources can even be beneficial. For example, if you are writing a paper about objectivity in the media, finding biased news articles might help support your argument. Being able to tell the different between useful bias and bias that will harm your paper is a crucial part of evaluating sources.

The following is a list of questions to consider when evaluating a source for biases:

- **Is the source a primary or a secondary source?** If a primary source is biased, it is usually less of a hindrance than a biased secondary source. Biased firsthand accounts are generally still usable, and little can be done about bias in this case unless multiple firsthand accounts exist. *For more information on primary and secondary sources, reference the respective sidebars in this chapter.*

- **Does the author admit to a bias or a particular lens?** Sometimes, an author might admit a bias in a source. A literary critic, for example, who admits to using a particular critical lens, is admitting a bias. As long as you recognize this bias and it supports what you are saying without skewing facts, these sources are still useful. Biased information can also be used to highlight parts of an argument you disagree with and are refuting in your paper. Pointing out the bias of a source that says the opposite of what you believe can be a great persuasive tool. You can also present an opinion from a different lens and then explain why you do not agree based on your research.

- **Does the bias help support my paper?** As mentioned above, some biases — such as critical lenses — can be beneficial to research. As long as the information in the source can be verified in other sources as well, using a source like this is usually OK.

- **Is the source purposely misleading?** Even if the bias of a source supports what you are trying to say, sources that are purposely vague, misleading, or incomplete in order to paint a particular picture should be avoided. Even if the part of the article you use is factual, the source will make the research seem sloppy.

■ **Is the bias so overt that it calls the credibility of the source into question?** Even if the facts in a source are correct and verifiable, if a source is too biased, it will reflect poorly on your paper. Teachers might question the credibility of the source and of your own work by proxy.

Tip No.

28 Learn the difference between acceptable and unacceptable bias.

Everyone has biases, but just as there is a difference between people who are so prejudiced they let their bias color their entire view of the world and people who simply have opinions or preferences, there are differences between biases found in sources. When the bias is mild, it can help support your theory. When it is strong, the information can be skewed. Unless you are writing a paper about bias, avoid the strongly biased sources.

In the end, always use your best judgment when evaluating for bias. There are exceptions to every rule, but you always want to use the best sources possible in your research paper. The quality of sources will affect the quality of your finished product. Showing that you know how to find and use good, credible sources will also impress teachers. If a source seems fishy or your gut tells you it might not be the best source you can find, keep looking until you find a better one.

Common Unreliable Sources

Here is a quick cheat sheet to use when trying to spot unreliable sources. Avoid or be highly skeptical of the following:

- **Wiki sites:** Wikipedia is not the only user-created encyclopedia out there. They come on a variety of topics. If the word "Wiki" appears anywhere in the link or the title, avoid it.

- **Personal websites:** These are almost always biased, so unless it is the personal website of a scholar on your topic, be suspicious.

- **Parody sites:** Several parody news sites have cropped up and can look exactly like real news websites. The Onion (**www.theonion. com**) is a great example of this. It seems obvious, but a surprising number of students find parody articles and mistake them for real news.

- **Fictionalizations/Dramatizations:** This goes for websites and print sources. Be on the look out for any disclaimers that say things such as "based on a true story" or "dramatization" because oftentimes these reports on events will take liberties with the truth.

Other things to consider

Beyond just evaluating for bias and credibility, there are a few other things to consider while researching and selecting sources. Consider which types of sources will be most useful to your research, and start there. Depending on the requirements placed upon you by your teacher, as well as the type of paper you are writing, you might need a certain number of primary or secondary sources as part of your research. *For more information on primary versus secondary sources, see the primary sources and secondary sources sidebars in this chapter.* You might also have an idea, depending on your topic, whether you will need more of a particular type of source. There might be a wide range of books or journal articles on your topic, or you might know that you will need lots of pictures or charts. If this is the case, start your search there, and then branch out.

Do not forget to think about the appropriateness of a particular source for your paper. A children's book about chemistry might be a great source for a paper about teaching elementary education, but it would be inappropriate for an AP Chemistry paper. Some classes and topics might require more formal sources, whereas some teachers might be comfortable allowing you to use blogs and comic strips as part of your research. On the opposite end of the spectrum, sources that are too technical can be inappropriate, as well. Some sources might be above the level of research expected for the project you are working on, which can be just as bad as using sources that are too simplistic. If there is so much jargon in the paper that you do not fully comprehend every aspect of the source, you might misuse it. Make sure every source you use is the perfect fit for the type of paper you are writing.

Tip No. **29** Understand primary and secondary sources and when to use them.

Some topics might use mostly primary sources, such as papers comparing pieces of literature or a history paper when there are several firsthand accounts available, but secondary sources are far more common. Think about the topic, and decide whether primary sources will be useful or necessary, and plan your research accordingly.

Finally, be sure to ask for help while searching for the best sources. Teachers are usually well-versed in almost every aspect of the subjects they teach. Most of them are usually more than happy to offer advice and sometimes will even give names or locations of good sources to use. Librarians are also helpful when doing research. Not only can they help locate books on your topic, but many librarians are also familiar with online databases, periodicals, and any other potential sources the library has access to. School librarians, especially, are accustomed to helping students with research projects and might even be familiar with your class or teacher. Other students can also be a huge help, so do not be afraid to ask your friends or classmates for assistance. You might find you know people who have already taken the class you are in right now or have done research on your topic for a different class. They might have some great ideas for where to find awesome sources.

Primary Sources

Primary sources are firsthand accounts of information without additional interpretation. Primary sources are often, but not always, less biased than secondary sources because they generally contain raw facts without another researcher's view coloring them. This does not necessarily make them better — just different. Depending on the topic, primary sources might be difficult to come by. Some examples of primary sources are:

- Raw research data from experiments
- Original works of fiction
- Statistics
- Recordings or transcriptions
- Letters/correspondences
- Diaries/journals
- Photographs or other images
- Eye witness accounts
- Government records

Secondary Sources

Secondary sources are the result of analyzing primary sources — and sometimes other secondary sources — or are sources written by people without firsthand experience. In these sources, other researchers analyze data gathered and draw conclusions based on their interpretations of that data. These interpretations will be slanted based on the viewpoint of the individual researcher, though some will be more biased than others. This does not make them worse than primary sources, and occasionally, this bias can help prove a point, rather than make researching more difficult. However, be aware of biases in any sources. Some examples of secondary sources are:

- Biographies
- Critical reviews
- Reviews or analysis of scientific studies
- Journal articles
- Encyclopedias
- Text books
- Most books and news articles

Using the Library

The library is an excellent starting place for any research project. Many students underestimate how useful libraries really are, especially with a new generation of students entering high school who are more familiar  with using the Internet to find the answers to most of their questions. There is a time and a place for Internet research, but most teachers require students to use at least some book references as a part of their research. As such, become familiar with your school or local library and all that it has to offer. Most libraries not only house thousands of books on hundreds, if not thousands, of topics, but they also have periodicals, journals, and online information databases. All of these things are indispensable while doing research. Libraries are usually safe places to start researching, as well, because they tend to have large quantities of quality unbiased sources. That being said, do not assume that just because you found it in a library it is an excellent source. Always evaluate sources using the tips discussed earlier in this chapter.

Tip No. 30 Befriend your librarian.
Librarians are extremely useful partners to have while doing research. Most of them know the libraries they work in inside and out, and they might even have suggestions for sources to look into. Teachers and students are helpful, too, but librarians spend the most time using the sources you are interested in, so do not dismiss how useful they can be

Using books, references, and periodicals

Each library is a little bit different, but most libraries have shelves full of hard copy books and reference books, and many libraries also have hard copies of periodicals. Looking at all of the resources available can be a little intimidating, but finding the materials you need has never been easier. Computers have made messy card catalogs a thing of the past. Your library likely has several computers set up to allow you to search for books by title, author, and keyword. There are also usually plenty of librarians and library assistants there to help you search and locate materials if you are having trouble locating a particular section.

Unless you already know a few titles you want to include in your research, starting things off with a keyword search is generally the best way to find lots of information quickly. Try searching several different words or phrases related to your subject and see what pops up. Write down the names and locations within the library of any books that look promising. Most digital catalogs include summaries, publication dates, and many other useful facts about the books listed in your search results, so pay attention to these. Many catalogs also list the keywords associated with each of their books, so if you find a book that sounds like it will be useful, see what other keywords are associated with it and try searching these for additional books. You might also want to check whether the same author has published any other books on the same subject. It is likely you will find more books dealing with your broad topic, rather than your narrow topic, so keep this in mind. Many books might only have a chapter or two that pertain directly to what you are researching. This is to be expected, but always choose the books from your search that have the most useful information related directly to your narrow topic.

On top of regular books, most libraries have a vast section of reference books, such as encyclopedias. For long papers or in-depth research papers, these types of sources are usually much too broad to be of real use. An encyclopedia is a great way to read a quick overview of your subject, as well as any related subjects you want to better acquaint yourself with. Doing this can help you come up with additional keywords to include in your search for subject-specific materials. Depending on your subject, you might also find a reference book, or several, specific to your topic. An example of this might be an encyclopedia of plants or a dictionary of scientific terms. References such as these can be useful to have on hand while doing research so you can look up any unfamiliar terms or jargon cropping up in the other sources you find.

In addition to books, most libraries subscribe to a list of periodicals, such as newspapers and scholarly journals. These are wonderful resources for research because they might have articles that deal explicitly with your topic, as opposed to books that cover a broader range of information you will have to pick through. Sometimes, these are searchable and included in the catalog; other times, they are not. To save yourself the trouble of searching through piles of magazines and journals, ask a librarian whether he or she has an indexed archive of the library's periodicals or a way to search them. If you tell the librarian your research topic, he or she will likely be able to point you toward a few journals or magazines that deal with your topic.

Periodicals

A periodical is any publication that comes out on a regular schedule. Newspapers, magazines, and journals are all examples of periodicals. The short articles found in periodicals are likely to cover smaller topics than books, so the chances of finding articles specifically about your topic are pretty good. Many periodicals are making the switch to online formats, however, and many libraries have switched periodical archives for online databases. The information you will find will be similar; the format is just different

If the library does not have a way to search its periodicals by subject or keyword, many publications have websites that allow you to search their archives. Once you know what issues of a periodical have articles pertaining to your topic, you can find out whether your library still has a copy on file. Because indexing periodicals can be such a time-consuming process, many libraries have stopped keeping archived periodicals or have limited how far back their archives go. If you are having trouble finding articles pertaining to your topic or your library does not have a large collection of periodicals, do not worry. Many libraries have started to replace their periodical selection with online databases because they are easier to keep up-to-date, are easier to search, and have access to a much larger quantity of information.

Tip No.

31 **With research, start narrow and then expand.**
When researching, take the opposite approach the book suggested when picking a topic. When picking a topic, the book suggests starting broad with the prewrite and then working down to a narrow topic. Now, in order to find the most applicable information possible, start your search with as narrow parameters as possible. Use specific keywords and criteria. Expand the search as needed to turn up more information, but the more specific you stay to the topic, the more appropriate information you are likely to find.

Using Online Library Databases

Online library databases are probably one of the best sources of articles from scholarly journals and periodicals to which you will have access. Most high schools pay a fee to subscribe to several databases, and some even provide login information so you can access them from home or school. Searching a database is much like searching the Internet for information, but the hits returned in a search will be articles published in journals or elsewhere. Sometimes, you might even find excerpts from books and other sources on these databases. Several types of online databases exist, covering a wide variety of subjects, so no matter what topic you are researching, you will likely find useful information.

Online Academic Databases

Academic databases are different from generic search engines. Schools, libraries, and other organizations generally pay a fee to subscribe to these databases, which contain articles from academic journals, archives, periodicals, and other sources. They save time because they contain more usable information than generic search engines and you do not have to sift through commercial websites when using a database.

How to select and search online databases

Your library will likely have information posted about how to access the online databases to which they subscribe. There might be printed instructions available with information about them or simply a page on  the library's website with information. If you are having trouble locating this information, ask a librarian for information about the library's online databases. In most cases, there will be a way to access the list of databases from a computer in the library, and usually each database the library subscribes to will have a small blurb about what sort of information it covers. Pay attention to these snippets so you do not waste time on a scientific journal database if you are doing an art history paper, or vice versa.

Tip No. 32 Research what sorts of databases are available.
Search around, and find out what databases you have access to through your school and local library. Also, find out whether there are databases around that they do not subscribe to that might be useful. Sometimes, there are free databases available online. Determine whether you can find somewhere local that has access to any databases your school or local library does not.

There are databases covering topics from art and literature to science and technology. Some will cover only scholarly journals, while others will cover magazines and newspapers. There are also more generic, or less topic specific, ones. To make the best use of these databases, consider following these steps during your search:

1. **Find databases pertaining specifically to your topic, if possible.** Check the brief overview of the databases you have access to, or ask a librarian or your teacher for recommendations. For example, if you are doing a science paper, there will likely be at least one scientific database. There might even be a more specific database available, such as one pertaining specifically to medical research, which could be helpful for a biology paper about cancer.

2. **Set up the search parameters within the database to be as narrow as possible.** To get the most pertinent information, determine what options are available to narrow your search. Often, you can narrow your search to only include articles within a specific date range or even uncheck certain types of journals and magazines that might be included in the database but have nothing to do with your topic. Also, use the most specific keywords possible when starting a search.

3. **Slowly expand your search to get additional results.** Likely, your specific search will return few results. This is good because these results will be easier to sift through and are likely to be current and applicable. If you do not get enough sources, slowly start to expand your date range, expand the types of journals you are searching, and use broader keywords to get more results.

4. **Move to the next database or a more general database if need be.** Once you have thoroughly searched one database, feel free to move to another to find more or better results. Some databases that cover the same topics might return some of the same

results, but you might find you prefer the search system of one over another, or they might actually cover radically different journals and archives. You can move to a more general database, as well, to determine whether that returns better results.

Another thing to consider while searching databases, or any scholarly publication for that matter, is the difference between peer-reviewed articles and other scholarly journals. You might notice that some articles are marked as peer-reviewed or that some databases allow you to search for only peer-reviewed articles. Peer-reviewed articles were written by an expert in a particular field and then reviewed by other experts, or peers, for quality before publication. Peer-reviewed journals, sometimes referred to as refereed journals, will only publish articles that pass the review stage. Articles from these sources are especially great because they can save you from checking whether other experts in the field approve of the information in the article. Scholarly articles that are not peer-reviewed are still fine as sources, but spend a little time evaluating the quality and bias of the article. If it is not clear whether the article was peer-reviewed, do a little research on the publication the database got it from and determine whether they are a peer-reviewed publication.

Tip No.

33 Print your articles from online sources.

Whether you find them on a database or elsewhere on the web, *always* print any articles you find and are planning to use as research. This will make them easier to annotate and ensure you have all the information needed to cite the source. It will also make it easier for you to find the source again, if need be. You might want to consider bookmarking any online sources in your Web browser for later reference as well.

Using the Internet

In addition to simply using the library for research, the Internet is a great — and sometimes terrible — additional tool to have at your disposal. The sheer volume of information available at the click of a button makes the Internet valuable in any research project. Most modern high school students also grew up using the Internet and turn to it to answer most of their questions, so using the Internet for research is almost second nature. The amount of information out there can be more of a hindrance than a help, sometimes, when students are forced to pick through thousands, or even millions, of hits for useful information. The fact that the Internet also makes it easy to anonymously publish nearly any sort of information without any filter also brings some of the credibility of Internet resources into question.

Types of websites

There are several types of websites floating around the Internet, and generally, the easiest way to distinguish them is by their URL tag (the letters after the dot at the end of a Web address). Here is a quick rundown on some of the most common URL tags and what they mean:

- **.com:** The com stands for "commercial." This tag is most commonly used for businesses or groups with a commercial interest.

- **.net:** Short for "network." This was originally meant to be used by information networks, or groups involved in information technology. Many people use it as an alternative to ".com."

- **.org:** Short for "organization," the intended use for this tag was noncommercial groups not fitting any of the other tags, but it is often used for personal websites and nonprofit organizations, among others.

- **.edu:** Short for "educational," this tag generally denotes a school, either grade or post-secondary.
- **.gov:** Short for "government," this tag is used by federal, state, and local government agencies in the United States.

Sites that end in either .edu or .gov are usually, but not always, kept up-to-date and will have accurate information. Educational websites might also have links to other sources they recommend, which can be a great way to jump-start your online research. Sites with other endings might also have useful information, but they are often less regulated. Almost anyone can register a website, and many free website services exist that allow anyone to make a professional-looking website and publish whatever they want on it. This brings this book to a point that is usually a hot-button issue between students and teachers, as well as within the academic world as a whole.

Wikipedia

Many teachers and educational institutions will specifically tell students not to use Wikipedia as a source — and for good reason. Wikipedia, for those unfamiliar, is an online user-run encyclopedia of information on an ever-growing list of subjects and has been around for more than a decade. An Internet search of just about anything will usually net a result from Wikipedia on the first page. Because it is run by an anonymous online community of users, however, it is often criticized for bias, having spoof articles, lack of citations, etc. Literally, anyone can get on and edit entries on the site, from qualified experts to bored high school students. Generally, articles on large or well-known topics are kept up-to-date and checked by moderators frequently, but things slip through the cracks. Articles can remain "flagged" for bias or lack of citations for months without being fixed, and often people fail to notice these tags on the articles or outright dismiss them.

Still, Wikipedia is the largest online encyclopedia around, and students still use it, even if they do not list it as a source in their papers. Students can use Wikipedia effectively when doing research; the issue is that many students do not know how to use it. References such as Wikipedia are good for getting a quick and gritty overview of an unfamiliar topic. More than likely, any article on Wikipedia will not go into enough depth or provide the type of information that is useful or appropriate in a high school-level research paper. Wikipedia can also be a great place to start looking for sources to use in your research because, in theory, any information on Wikipedia was researched by someone else and should be properly cited. If you choose to use Wikipedia, the following are a few do's and don'ts to keep in mind:

Do:

- Check to see what, if any, issues the article has been flagged for. These should be listed at the top of the article. Articles that have disputed neutrality or not enough citations should be treated as such.

- Check images, graphs, and other charts that might be found as part of the entry, as sometimes these are useful for gaining perspective on a research topic.

- Examine the sources listed at the bottom of the article. You might wind up using some of them as sources if they are of high enough quality.

Don't:

- Treat Wikipedia as a scholarly source. It is not, but it might point you in the direction of other scholarly sources in the citations section at the bottom of the article.

- Quote or paraphrase Wikipedia in a paper. Sometimes plagiarized information will appear on Wikipedia, and you do not want that in your paper. As previously mentioned, many teachers will not even allow Wikipedia as a source.

- Accept everything written on Wikipedia as true. Use your best judgment, and if something sounds fishy, investigate. This goes double for any claims that do not have a citation or are marked "citation needed."

Tip No. 34 **If you choose to start at Wikipedia, do not end at Wikipedia.** Wikipedia, like any reference, is an OK starting point. Do not end your search for resources there, though. Treat it as a jumping off point, not an ending place for research. It can help you find sources, but this does not make it a good source itself.

Using a blog as a resource

Blogs are becoming increasingly common in the Internet world. Short for "Web log," blogs are written by an author, or group of authors, and generally cover a specific topic. There are blogs on just about every topic, so it is entirely possible that there is a blog out there relating to your research topic. Many blogs are strongly opinionated and can lack the sort of professionalism one expects from a scholarly source. Blogs are not appropriate for every research paper and should probably be avoided in many cases. In some papers on contemporary or Internet-related topics, it might be appropriate to use a blog, especially now that many famous politicians and media personalities are blogging. As with any source, be sure to check the author's credentials, evaluate the blog for bias, and use common sense. Also, be aware of any affiliations the blog might have. Blogs also tend to be opinionated, so double- and triple-check all facts and figures presented to make sure you are not using skewed information in your paper as fact.

Blogs and Social Networking

Today, almost everyone has a blog and subscribes to several social networking websites. News organizations ask watchers to follow them on Facebook and Twitter. Blogs toe the line of acceptable resources, and anything posted on a social networking site should be avoided. Even if they are associated with big names or major news corporations, using these as sources does not look professional.

Determining trustworthiness of Internet information

This chapter has already spent a lot of time on determining the credibility and quality of sources, but students must be especially wary of the credibility of online sources, so it is worth mentioning again. Always approach online sources skeptically and fact check any information you choose to use from a Web source. Most websites on the Internet have not undergone the editing and fact-checking processes that most traditional publishers require, so people can literally make up false information and present it as fact online. These websites can even look and sound legitimate, so be cautious and alert for anything that throws up a red flag.

The following are a few Internet-specific rules to keep in mind while evaluating potential online sources:

- **Check for the authorship of online information.** With the exception of statistics pulled from government websites that might not list a specific author, you never want to use an anonymous online source. If they did not want their name associated with it, it is probably not worth using.

- **Look for the date the website was last updated.** It can be difficult to determine how long a website has been active, and it might have been unattended for years or just contain outdated information. Oftentimes, there will be a note at the top or bottom of the page with this information, or on larger websites, it might be under an "about this page" section. There might also be a copyright date, which will also give you an idea of the age of the information. If this information cannot be located, consider finding another source, or try to verify the information with other sources.

- **Try to verify any credentials an author claims to have.** The anonymity of the Web makes it easy for people to say they have degrees and certifications they do not. Search the author online, see if they have a personal website, and check for other pieces they might have written for reputable publishers. Sometimes this can be difficult and daunting, but just try to keep an eye out for anything that seems suspicious, and trust your instincts. You can also run sources past tutors or teachers for a second opinion if you are really unsure.

- **Check for citations when they seem necessary.** Plagiarism runs rampant on the Internet, and you will often find multiple websites with the exact same information, word for word, with no way of telling who the original author was. If a website does not offer any sources, be suspicious.

In the end, use your head and your best judgment, and remember, if something seems suspicious, it probably is.

CASE STUDY: A SCIENCE TEACHER'S PERSPECTIVE

Name: Joy Kizior
Company: Racine Unified
School District
Job Title: Teacher

I am a first year teacher, so I have written many papers during my own education, plus I have edited and graded high school papers for several classes.

A good paper should have continuity of thought and details: quotes, specific data, or pictures. Before beginning, I recommend that students make an outline of their thesis and main points. The easiest things to write about are things you are interested in, so even if the topic is predetermined, try to put your own interests in the thesis; keep yourself motivated to do the research.

Writing is not always easy. I have struggled with thesis statements myself, and I teach science, which has a more formulaic approach to forming a thesis. I think a good thesis statement should connect the ideas the writer is about to explain without being a laundry list.

Such as: poison dart frogs gain their unique coloration as a result of their natural toxins.

Instead of: poison dart frogs are very colorful because the pigments in their skin are acidic, they do not need camouflage, and this is a shared trait of other poisonous life forms.

I have also struggled with introductions; it is difficult to make an introduction that pulls the reader in or carries a theme throughout a paper. There is a delicate balance of creative presentation and factual presentation in a good research paper; often a good balance is there when the writer cares about the topic, but tricky in assigned papers.

A general place to start is why the writer is bothering to do this research in the first place. For instance, poison dart frogs are the only red and blue frogs in the whole world. Interesting observations lead to interesting questions. Why are they the only ones? Do all of their predators see in color? Etc.

Saying that poison dart frogs are blue because of a unique arsenic compound in their skin is linking their color to their poisonous properties. This supports the thesis, and is a fact that can be expanded upon; who isolated the poison, how do we know it's blue, and it is bad for camouflage in the frog's natural environment.

For finding literary support, librarians can be very helpful. For online information I prefer going to an expert in the area, such as The American Chemical Society, U.S. Food and Drug Administration, Brown County Historical Society, or janeausten.org.

I consider online sources on which you can find all of the citation information easily a fairly good judge of reliability. Note the difference among '.com,' '.org,' '.edu,' and '.html,'

I outline in MS Word; whenever I find information I want to use in my paper, I get the quote and cite my source where I want to use it in my outline. I build the works cited as I go, and I can paraphrase or look up more information later if I need to.

Giving credit where credit is due is important for its own sake. Furthermore, plagiarism is illegal. Your high school teacher may not send you to jail, but he or she can lower your grade, throw out your whole paper, and make a note on your permanent record if the plagiarism is chronic.

Keeping track of your sources is good if the focus of your paper changes, you lose your work, or you need more information.

I think good teachers should have supportive due dates: first your topic and thesis, next your outline, then your introduction, then some cited sources, then your support, and finally your whole paper. Good papers, unfortunately for time management, need to be reviewed and rewritten. When you do not have a good teacher, you can do the chunking yourself. (i.e. don't expect to get it all done in one night, and it's not healthy if you do it that way.)

Study Guide

❑ Finding credible sources is crucial to a research paper. You only want to use the best sources for any paper, so make sure to examine any source carefully.

❑ Do not assume that just because information is in print somewhere it is accurate. Double- and triple-check any source for false claims, bias, and loaded or vague words.

❑ Look into what other people are saying about a source or the author of the source, as well as any organizations the author or source might be affiliated with.

❑ Become acquainted with your school or local library, as well as the people who work there. They will be able to help you find books, reference materials, periodicals, and more.

❑ Periodicals, magazines, and journals are great for finding specific information on your topic, as many books will cover much broader topics with limited useful information. If the library does not have many of these on hand, check the online databases to which they subscribe.

❑ When searching online databases, or anywhere else, always start your search as narrow as possible. and then slowly broaden the search parameters to find more sources as needed.

❑ The Internet can be a great source of information, but be sure to check URL tags and the sources behind any information found online.

❑ Wikipedia can be a starting point for research, but approach anything on there with a grain of salt, as anyone can edit it.

❑ Always be wary of any online information, especially anonymous or improperly cited sources. Be suspicious — it will save you a headache later.

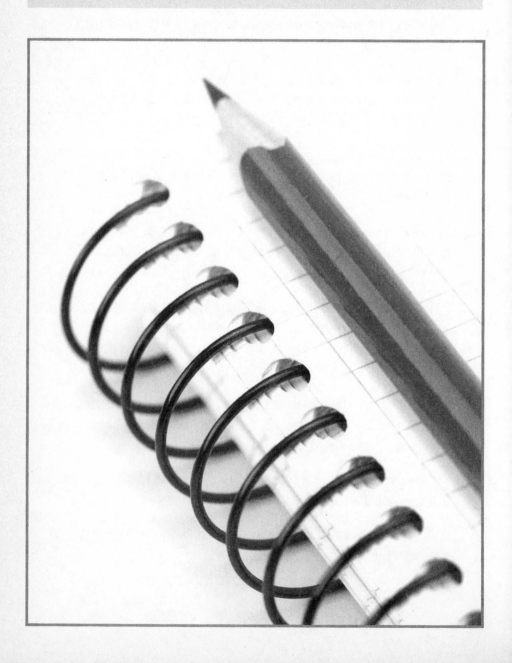

CHAPTER 6:

Organizing and Outlining

Once the research is done, the next step is organizing all of that information. More than likely, you now have several sources to pick through and decide how best to use them. It is intimidating to look at, and it can be difficult to see how all of this information will fit together into a coherent research paper. That is where this chapter comes in. Now that you have collected all of this information, you need to find a way to organize it. There are many options for organizing your information. This chapter will discuss a few different options, so feel free to try multiple methods to find what works best. As with prewriting, you can even make up your own organizational methods as long as they help you keep track of all of your sources and create an outline for your paper. An outline will save you time while writing, and if you do not keep track of your sources, doing citations and a bibliography for the paper will be a nightmare.

Organizing Information and Sources

Whether you use notecards, take notes, or use more digital means, such as spreadsheets, you will need to keep track of all of the information for your paper, as well as where it is coming from. There is nothing more frustrating than having to dig through piles of information to find one or two sentences you were planning to quote in your paper but not being able to remember where that information came from. In order to save time later, the following section describes a few different methods for organizing the quotes, paraphrases, and other information you want to reference while writing your paper.

Notecards

Using notecards is probably the most common method of keeping track of information. Many teachers espouse their use early on, so many students are comfortable using them once they reach high school and beyond. Other students find them time-consuming and tedious. Often, this is because they do not understand how to effectively make notecards. Notecards are cheap and easy to find in most general stores. Some schools even keep basic supplies like this on site for student use.

The most basic notecards will include the following:

- A quotation, paraphrase, or relevant piece of information
- The page number (if applicable) or general location of this information within the source
- Citation information for the source (at least the title and author)

You can include more information if you desire, but these basics should always be added. Often, it is useful to put the relevant information on one side of the notecard, along with the page number or a description of where in the document this information is located. On the back of the card, write the title, author, or a complete citation if it helps you.

Tip No. 35 Keep your notecards (and other notes) organized.
Color-coding or using other methods to keep notecards separate is a great way to help keep your notes organized. Longer papers might require stacks of notecards, so trying to find a specific one in a pile of a hundred is time-consuming as well as frustrating. Also, consider investing in some rubber bands to keep notecards together so you do not lose any while shuffling papers or moving from one location to another.

When making notecards, it is also useful to consider how you would like to organize the notecards themselves. Some students prefer to keep all of their notecards from a particular source together. For the purposes of making an outline, however, it is often useful to organize the notecards by subtopic. Take a look at the supporting points you included in your thesis statement, and break this up into points you wish to cover in your paper. Then, divide the notecards up by the points they best support. You might wish to assign numbers to specific categories or maybe even use highlighters or markers to color-code the notecards so they are easy to keep separate. This will also make finding specific notecards much easier when it comes time to make an outline or write that part of the paper.

Tip No. 36 Even if you are not a "note taker," force yourself to write down some notes.

Did you know that when you write something down, your brain stores the information in a different location from when you read it? This is what makes taking notes so useful, even if you do not go back over your notes later. Just the act of writing down information makes you more likely to remember it because you are storing it in two places in your brain. This is the natural equivalent of saving a backup copy of your work on your computer. If you want to make remembering information even easier, try reading your notes out loud to yourself after you have copied them down. You might feel goofy doing it, but it will further reinforce the memory.

Notecard example

Here is a sample notecard. Feel free to use this as a template for your own notecards, or design your own method.

Front:

```
Topic: Media Attention and Growth

Despite the recession, the criminal
justice field is still potentially
growing, especially in the area of
forensic science. This is largely
because of public interest and media
attention due to the popularity of TV
crime dramas.

                              pp. 3
```

Back

John M. Doe. "The Rise of Forensic
Science in Popular Culture"

Article from Criminal Justice and
Forensic Science Monthly

Notecards in the Digital Age

In the age of the Internet, many students prefer to use their computers for almost everything. Using digital means to organize information is handy because it is neat, digital files are usually searchable, and copy/paste functions make dropping in quotes and notations easy. If paper notecards are not for you, try typing up notes in a word document or spreadsheet. Spreadsheets are easy to use and a great way to organize information so it can be found quickly. Make columns in the spreadsheet with the data, citation information, and whatever other information you choose to include. This should allow you to sort the spreadsheet by any of these columns, which makes looking for information by topic or author easy.

If you do not have Excel or another spreadsheet program on your computer, you can download a free bundle of word processing programs from OpenOffice.org. Another alternative would be using the "Create Table" function in your word processing program to organize your information and what source it is coming from. There are also several programs available, both commercially and as freeware, that are designed to help students keep track of notes, so if you want to go digital but are intimidated by spreadsheets, you might want to consider researching what other programs are available.

Developing An Outline

By now, you should have done enough research to construct an outline for your paper. Odds are good that while you were reading through sources, making notecards or spreadsheets, or even brainstorming, you started to create an outline in your head, possibly without realizing it. Most students will stop there, organizing their thoughts in their heads without actually committing them to paper. It is easy to scoff at outlines as a waste of time when you are on a tight deadline, but the truth of the matter is that outlines are invaluable tools that are crucial in writing an impressive paper. They usually even turn out to be time savers in the long run as well.

Tip No. **37** Find a trick to force yourself to outline, such as using a reward system.

Most students procrastinate the most on projects they are dreading or on parts of projects that give them the most trouble. This procrastination wastes precious time and can result in students simply skipping the outlining in an attempt to buy more time to work on the rest of the paper. Never forget that this step will save you time later, so if you are a student who hates outlining, find something to force yourself to complete it. Give yourself a treat for completing an outline, or ban yourself from playing games or watching TV until you finish your outline. If you have friends who are also working on papers, plan an outlining party. Give yourself a reason to look forward to the writing process, and then reward yourself for a job well done.

Why developing an outline is important

As stated in Chapter 4, your thesis statement is the paper's road map. Think of your research paper as a road trip. The thesis provides the direction, or final destination, and should give you an idea of what major stops you will make along the way. The outline is a complement to the thesis statement and acts more like a trip's itinerary. An itinerary outlines each stop on a trip, what activities are planned, and how much time will be spent at each location. Similarly, an outline should list out each of your major points, list what information will be included with each point, and also give you an idea of how much space each section of the paper will take up.

Tip No. 38 Your notecards will go hand in hand with your outline.

Outlines and notecards complement each other well. You can reference notecards by number in your outline or lay out your notecards on the floor or a large table while constructing your outline. These tools should mesh together so you never have to sit and figure out what comes next while writing your paper. If you are a visual person and you like the idea of a quotation outline (which will be discussed later in the chapter), you can turn your notecards directly into an outline by marking them up and putting them in the order they will be referenced in your paper or taping them to a large board or piece of paper with notations.

Once you have gone to all the trouble of organizing your research materials and finding supporting information for you paper — be it by using notecards, a spreadsheet, or a different method entirely — you need to figure out how it all fits together in your paper. If you do not know where and how the information fits with your argument, having all the notes in the world will be like having a bunch of disassembled puzzle pieces. Many students avoid outlines much the same way many avoid prewriting, but this step in the planning process is a huge time saver and will help you avoid staring at a blank screen for hours trying to come up with what to write next. Outlines also are extremely helpful tools for remembering important information when it comes time to actually write the paper. Without an outline, students often find themselves rambling or meandering away from the point of their paper without meaning to or even realizing it. Outlines eliminate much of the guesswork from the writing process.

How to construct an outline

There are multiple strategies for constructing an outline, and they can range from loose notes or charts to rigidly detailed lists. Some types of outlines will lend themselves better to certain types of papers than others. A short research paper might only need a brief outline or flowchart to serve as a reminder for what order to cover key points in, while long research papers or science reports will likely require a more detailed outline to help stay on track. Just as there is really no wrong way to prewrite, there is really no wrong way to write an outline for a paper so long as it gets the job done. Try different outlines, and see what helps you with your writing process the most. You might find one way of outlining that does the trick every time or develop multiple strategies for tackling papers on different subjects.

Just keep in mind that a good working outline will likely include the following information:

- Your paper's thesis statement
- Each of your paper's key points
- The order the key points will be addressed in
- References to your research and what sources will be included where

39 An "outline" does not have to be in the format of a traditional outline.

If you are a more right-brained thinker and the thought of rigid outlines gives you a headache, consider making a flowchart instead. You can even make an idea web and then assign an order to each section of the web. Get some poster board and tape all of your notecards to it, divided by topic. Get a stack of post-it notes and write down all the points you want to cover in your paper and then stick them up on the wall and rearrange them until you are pleased with the order. If your outline does not have bullet points or Roman Numerals but it helps you organize your paper's key points, it is still an outline!

The following sections will provide you with a more complete understanding of how to construct three different types of outlines. This is by no means an exhaustive list of outlining methods, and these methods can be mixed, matched, and altered to better suit your purposes. Just remember: as long as it saves time and helps you write a better paper, you are doing it correctly.

Topic Outline

The topic outline is what most students think of when they hear the word "outline." This is seen by many as the "traditional" outline and is simple in nature. A topic outline lists out each topic, without many details, and includes any relevant subtopics below each topic. A topic outline generally looks something like this:

Sample topic outline

I.   Introduction

    A. Thesis Statement: Although the glamorous portrayal of criminal justice work in pop culture might increase the number of students studying this important field, it ultimately hurts the profession by flooding the job market with misinformed individuals who do their jobs incorrectly and do not enjoy the work.

II. High Dropout/Failure Rates

    A. Spike in program applicants compared to popularity of crime dramas on TV

    B. Statistics for GPA and Dropout rate

III. Flooded Job Market

    A. Shifts in competitiveness of job market

    B. Reality Check for number of open positions in real life vs. TV

IV. Impact on the Field

    A. Fantasy vs. Reality

        B. Changes in field since surge in
           crime drama TV

        C. Satisfaction of graduates/workers

    V.   Conclusion

The thesis statement is the only complete sentence in the outline. Everything else is rough and loose. If this sample were a real outline, it would also include some notations for where some of the referenced statistics are located, an author and page number or a notecard number, for example. If you like this format but require more detail, you can include points under each sub-point and so on. This type of outline is an excellent choice for people who do not like to outline because it is easy to construct and consists of a few brief notes to set up the flow of information. The great thing is that it can work equally well for long and short papers and you can add as much, or as little, detail as you feel necessary.

Tip No. **40** Focus on the order, not the details.
The outlining stage, though more detail-oriented than the previous writing exercises covered in this book so far, is not the time and the place to get hung up on the specifics. If you are not positive about all you would like to say on a topic you know you want to include, that is OK. The most important thing is finding a logical progression for your argument. Setting the order that points will be addressed is the real goal, not planning out everything said. You can always readdress the order if new ideas present themselves during the writing process. For now, just focus on giving yourself signposts to follow while writing.

Sentence Outline

Another common type of outline is the sentence outline. A sentence outline is similar to a topic outline, but rather than just roughly listing out each topic without any details, each point and sub-point is a complete sentence. Sentence outlines require a bit more thought than topic outlines, but they have the benefit of generally being much more detailed. Another great benefit is that while you will be putting more work into the outline, the sentences you craft as part of the outline can often be copied directly into that part of the paper, with or without some minor edits. Here is how the same example used in the previous section would look as a sentence outline:

Sentence outline sample

```
I. The introduction of the paper will
   move from the broad ways in which the
   entertainment industry shapes our
   lives to how specifically the recent
   popularity of crime dramas has changed
   the face of criminal justice.

   A. Although the glamorous portrayal
      of criminal justice work in pop
      culture might increase the number
      of students studying this important
      field, it ultimately hurts the
      profession by flooding the job
      market with misinformed individuals
      who do their jobs incorrectly and
      do not enjoy the work.
```

II. In recent years, the dropout rates
    have risen and GPAs have suffered
    in secondary programs related to
    criminal justice.

    A. Studying criminal justice is
       seen as glamorous due to the
       romanticized portrayal of the field
       on television.

    B. More students than ever are
       enrolling in these programs with
       little idea what they are actually
       getting themselves into.

    C. Statistics show that the dropout
       rate has gone up in recent years
       as well.

III. Due to the rise in graduates with
     criminal justice degrees, the
     job market has become flooded
     with applicants.

    A. Many of these applicants are
       misinformed about the field and
       what their job responsibilities
       will be.

    B. The competitive nature of the
       field makes landing even low level

positions difficult, let alone "glamorous" ones.

IV.   Despite the fact that many of these shows try to check their facts, the characterization that lends to great drama does not accurately imitate how real police forces and crime labs are organized.

   A. The influx of graduates, media attention, and Hollywood interest in criminal justice has had an impact on the field.

   B. In some ways, much of what is seen on TV is a fantasy that real life will never be able to imitate, though there are some ways the attention has changed the field for the better.

V.   Greater public interest inevitably leads to better funding and research.

   A. Public attention is also bad in many aspects as crime dramas may lead to smarter, or better-informed, criminals coupled with misinformed workers.

B. Job satisfaction has also been
   affected by the romanticized
   version of crime drama seen
   on television.

VI.   The conclusion will start off with a
      restated thesis and then address the
      ways in which crime drama has shaped
      the criminal justice field as well
      as offer solutions for how it could
      work to improve the field rather than
      damage it.

Tip No. 41

Think about topic sentences while crafting a sentence outline.

When it comes time to write the body of your paper, each paragraph will need to have a topic sentence. Think of the topic statement as a miniature thesis statement. This sentence should define what the paragraph will cover. If you keep this fact in mind while putting together sentences in your outline, you will likely find that many of the sentences you have written will become the topic sentences for the paragraphs in your body. If you take a little extra time now to make sure these sentences are well written, you will save yourself time later because you can import them directly into your paper.

Quotation Outline

The last type of outline this chapter will cover is the quotation outline. A quotation outline is a bit different from the previous two outlines and is particularly useful for papers that require a lot of sources. When the backbone of your paper will involve statistics from research or quotes from a book that need to be analyzed, it can be difficult to determine how to lead from one quote, paraphrase, or statistic to the next. Quotation outlines are almost like a combination of notecards and outlines. In this type of outline, you arrange quotes, statistics, and other information you will be using in your paper so they progress logically to support the paper's thesis. You can then build up information around these quotes in order to link them together and so that they flow neatly with your argument. Even if you are not planning on paraphrasing the information in the quote, include it with citation information as well as notes on how the quote supports your argument.

Tip No. 42 Quotation outlines can include more than just quotations, despite what the name might imply.

Most frequently, you will find yourself simply using quotations at this stage because you have likely just copied quotes over from your notecards, but if you already have paraphrases or summaries in mind, you can include them in this type of outline. Tables, diagrams, and charts are fair game, as well. If you do not know for certain what information you will be quoting and what you will be paraphrasing yet, that is okay. Just use quotations for now and you can decide how to present the information within your paper later.

Here is a template you can follow when putting together a quote outline. This template uses a table format, but feel free to use a spreadsheet, bullet points, or a numbered outline if it makes you more comfortable.

Paper Title		
Thesis statement:	Notes/ideas for introduction.	
Supporting Point No. 1:	"Quotation From Source" Citation Information	This supports this point because...
	Relevant Statistic Citation Information	This supports this point because...

Supporting Point No. 2:	"Quotation From Source" Citation Information	This supports this point because...
	Paraphrase From Source Citation Information	This supports this point because...
Supporting Point No. 3:	Paraphrase From Source Citation Information	
	"Quotation From Source" Citation Information	
	Paraphrase From Source Citation Information	
Notes/ideas for conclusion.		

This template can be edited to suit the needs of your paper. You might have more supporting points and the number of quotes, paraphrases, and statistics you include under each point will vary based on your paper and what sort of information you are planning on using. Change the template to suit your needs. So long as you list out your points and the supporting evidence you are using, as well as some notes on how it supports your argument, you have succeeded in making a quotation outline.

Tip No. 43 Save your strongest argument for last.
Before you call your outline complete, take a look at the order you have put your arguments in. Is your paper's final point before the conclusion a big one? If not, you might want to reconsider your order and see if the progression of ideas will be disrupted if you change your strongest point to your last. Your paper should gain momentum as it goes. Starting off with your strongest point and ending with your weakest might cause your paper to fizzle. Make sure you end with a bang rather than a pop. If you absolutely cannot change the order you are addressing your points in, try to find some extra support for your last point and strengthen it as much as possible.

Study Guide

❏ One you have done all of your research, organizing it is vital. Good organization saves time later as well as raises your chances of constructing a well-written paper.

❏ Notecards are a great way to organize your sources.

> ❏ Only put one quote, statistic, or piece of information on each card.
> ❏ Be sure to include citation information on each notecard.
> ❏ Consider color-coding, numbering, or otherwise organizing the notecards so they are easy to navigate later.
> ❏ Keep notecards in a box or rubber band them together so they do not get lost.

❏ Computerized databases or spreadsheets can also be used to keep track of citation information for sources.

> ❏ These are useful because they are often searchable and can usually be organized by title, author, or whatever else works best for you.
>
> ❏ Quotes, statistics, and other information pulled from each source can be kept with the citation information for easy reference later.

❏ Constructing an outline is also vital and should not be skipped. Outlines save time later and provide a more detailed plan for writing your paper than a thesis statement alone.

❏ There are multiple types of outlines, but all should include:

> ❏ Your paper's thesis statement

❑ Each of your paper's key points
❑ The order the key points will be addressed in
❑ References to your research and what sources will be included where

❑ Topic outlines are basic and list out key points without a lot of detail.

❑ Sentence outlines are more detailed and will explain each point and sub-point as a complete sentence.

❑ Quotation outlines are a great way to organize information for papers that rely heavily on quoted or paraphrased reference material.

❑ There is no wrong way to organize information for your paper as long as it works for you, so experiment and find what works best for you and the type of paper you are writing.

CHAPTER 7

Plagiarism and Using Research in a Paper

Research papers require students to crawl through piles of potential sources to find support for their topics. Using these sources in the paper without plagiarizing them might seem like a bit of a conundrum to students who have not written many research papers. Plagiarism is a serious subject and should not be taken lightly. It is important to understand the difference between proper research and plagiarism. This chapter will explore what plagiarism is as well as what you can do to avoid it.

Plagiarism and its Consequences

Plagiarism is one of those words you will hear thrown around a lot within the academic community, particularly at the high school and college level. Some writing-heavy classes might even require students to sign anti-plagiarism agreements or run each of their assignments through plagiarism-detecting software. It is made clear that plagiarism is unacceptable. This idea might seem simple enough, but it can become a little tricky when it comes time for research papers. Often, students do not have a clear understanding of exactly what plagiarism is, so resolving the need to use sources and the need to not copy the work of others can seem impossible.

What is plagiarism?

To put it simply, plagiarism is taking someone else's words, ideas, or other intellectual property and passing it off as your own. Think of it as not giving credit where credit is due. Any time you borrow, copy, reference, summarize, paraphrase, or quote the work of another, you must give the original author credit or you will be committing plagiarism. This can seem daunting, but as long as your sources are properly organized, it really should not be a problem. This is why it is so important to organize your sources and write down page numbers, titles, and authors for later reference. You will use this information to give the original author credit in your work. As long as credit is properly given, there is no plagiarism. If you improperly give credit or forget to cite all of your sources, however, you can quickly find yourself in trouble.

Tip No. **44** Look into plagiarism-detecting utilities.
Your teacher might require you to run your paper through a plagiarism detector when you submit it, or he or she might run it through one after you have turned it in. As long as you have been careful about documenting and citing your sources, this should be no problem. Nonetheless, you might want to consider looking online for a free plagiarism scanner to run your paper through, just to make sure nothing pops up that you might have been unaware of. These are far from foolproof, but it does not take much time to run a scan, and doing it will not hurt anything.

The consequences

It is easy to dismiss plagiarism as something "other" students do. You might think students who plagiarize are unethical delinquent types who know they are breaking the rules but do it anyway. The truth is that plagiarism also springs from confusion, oversight, and laziness. There are plenty of students who deliberately plagiarize and hope they will get away with it. There are just as many who do not realize the seriousness of what they are doing or do not even realize that they are plagiarizing. Dropping in a few sentences in your paper and forgetting or losing the citation information can get you expelled. Plagiarism is theft, plain and simple. It is not only a question of ethics, but also a question of legality.

Tip No. 45 When in doubt, cite it!

If you ever pause for a moment and find yourself wondering if you need to use a citation for a piece of information or section of your paper, assume the answer is "Yes." The consequences are too great to take chances with this. Depending on the format the paper is in, the citations might seem time-consuming or make the paper look cluttered. Because citations are an integral part of research papers, as long as they are done properly, teachers will not see the paper as cluttered. Just remember, it is always worth the extra time, and academic writing is, with rare exceptions, full of citations.

Getting caught plagiarizing has serious consequences. Best case scenario, you might only fail the assignment or the class. Depending on your school's policies, however, you might find yourself expelled or facing legal action. The author you plagiarized from could file suit against you, and there are fines for violating copyright laws. Never assume no one will notice or that using a small idea or paraphrase without a citation is OK. It is not worth the consequences. If there is ever any question in your mind about whether or not something needs a citation, put one there. It might be difficult, time-consuming, or annoying, but the hassle is better than risking your education. Because of how important this is, the rest of this chapter will be spent discussing ways you can use your source materials, when to use them, and how to use them without plagiarizing.

Quoting vs. Paraphrasing vs. Summarizing

There are three ways to use your sources in your paper. Use this as a quick reference to understand the difference between quoting, paraphrasing, and summarizing, as well when each method should be used.

Quotations use the author's exact words as they are written in the source. All quotes should be surrounded by quotation marks so it is obvious they are quotations.

- Use quotes for particularly interesting and striking excerpts from your sources. When you find a section that makes you think "I could not have said this better myself," this is when to use a quote.

Paraphrases are different from quotations in that they do not use an author's exact words. Rather, you are taking the main ideas from a section of the author's work and putting it into your own words.

- Paraphrases are best used when you need to convey facts or details that you got from a source, but the author's own wording is not particularly striking or important. This is also a good way to highlight how this information applies specifically to your main points.

Summaries are similar to paraphrases but generally cover a broader section of the author's work. Summaries use ideas from a chapter or other large section of the source and are written in your own words.

- Summaries work best when you want to incorporate ideas from several different parts of the source into one sentence or a few sentences. Consider summaries when giving brief overviews of key facts that are needed to understand the core of your argument.

CASE STUDY: STRUGGLING WITH PAPERS

Name: William Canales
Job Title: Student

I am a high school student who has struggled academically, specifically with writing, in the past. I am dyslexic, so none of this has ever come easy for me. When I was in 6th grade, I was told I would never be able to write a full report. Two weeks later, I proved them wrong and accomplished just that. I found something interesting, and I built off it until I had a full report. Now I just find something interesting to latch onto in a paper to make it amusing. It helps me stay determined.

What separates a great paper from an okay paper is time, reasoning, and effort. If you are just starting high school, keep in mind that deadlines are much more strict. Also, errors in your paper — even tiny ones — can be marked wrong.

I recommend getting a comfy area to do research in. If the area you are in is not comfy, then make it more comfortable. Turn on some music or drink some coffee. What ever gets you in the zone. Block out all distractions, then you can view your research with interest.

You need to take all possible distractions and put them away. Prepare music to listen to ahead of time so you don't have to keep changing it, and make sure it's the kind of music you can listen to without getting distracted. Drink some coffee or tea, preferably something warm, to keep yourself comfortable.

Not everybody wants to write, but you will have to at some point. I recommend that you try acting like you enjoy it. If you expect there to be something fun or interesting about the project, it will be easier to stay focused and get it done. Don't force enthusiasm, find something you are already enthusiastic about and build off it. Take it one step at a time and things will fall into place.

Quoting

When most students think about using another author's material in their papers, using direct quotes is the first thing and the safest thing that comes to mind. Any time you use someone else's exact words in your paper, you are quoting them. It is important you treat these excerpts as quotations. They must be surrounded with quotation marks and cited. Some students make the mistake of putting everything that they cite into quotation marks to avoid plagiarism, despite the fact that summaries and paraphrases should not have quotation marks. It is important to make sure you do not change anything when presenting a quote in your paper. If you change the wording, it is not a quote, so putting it in quotation marks and treating it like the author's words is a misrepresentation. With web sources, it is often easiest to just copy and paste the quote directly into your document. If it is a print source, double-check to make sure you have typed the quote in correctly.

Tip No. 46   Make sure your quotes are actually quotes!
If it has quotation marks around it, readers will assume that it is the author's exact words. This means you need to have anything you quote correct, down to the last comma. If you need to omit part of a quote because it is not relevant and deleting it does not alter the meaning at all, use ellipsis to signal that something has been omitted. If you must change a word or words for the quote to make sense, use brackets to show that you have changed these words. This might be necessary if the quote uses pronouns and you are not quoting anything that shows what or whom the pronoun is referring to.

Another important point to keep in mind when using quotations is to make sure you are using them in the proper context. It is easy to twist someone else's words to fit your point when you remove the context. Make sure you have a full understanding of exactly what the author means in the quotation so you do not accidentally misrepresent it. Read the quotation as a stand-alone excerpt to make sure it still retains the same meaning. If it does not, be sure that you frame it properly in your paragraph, possibly using a paraphrase to lead into the quote in order to give it context so the reader understands what the quotation actually means.

When to use a quotation

Quotes are used to showcase a pertinent thought from another author. Students often make the mistake of overusing quotes. If the author's wording is not particularly striking, a paraphrase will often work better. When you do come across sentences that really grab your attention, are well-worded, and hit on a key point in your argument, then use a quote. Be sure to only include the most interesting and vital bits of information in the quotation. Students often make the mistake of quoting large sections of "fluff" when they really only needed one small point. Quotes can be long but oftentimes will only be a couple of sentences. Quotes can even be partial sentences. The most important thing to remember when deciding to use a quote is to make sure you pick sections of the author's work that add to your paper as they are written without having to edit or change any details.

Tip No.

47 Your quotes should showcase the best from the sources you have selected.

Ideally, you will feel that all of your sources are well-written, informative, and credible. *If not, you might want to refer back to Chapter 5.* Even if you feel that everything in a source is extremely on point and quotable, try to use quotations only for the absolute best points from a given source. This is your research paper, after all, and it should not read like a laundry list of quotations from other authors. Beginning writers often make the mistake of overusing quotations in their papers, so try not to use a quote when a paraphrase will do.

Citations and quoting

Quotations are likely the most straightforward type of support to cite. Quotations, due to their nature, have a definitive start and end as well as a specific location from which they were pulled. Placing a citation at the end of the quotation is rather easy, and generally a quote will come from a single page, possibly two. The citation, be it a parenthetical reference, footnote, or other annotation, will go directly after the terminal quotation mark. Parenthetical citations should always go before the period indicating the end of the sentence, though. If the quote falls in the middle of a sentence, place the citation where the quotation ends, even if it is in the middle of the sentence. It will take a bit to get use to seeing parenthetical citations in this manner, but do not worry. Footnotes or endnotes are less disruptive because they should only consist of a superscript number in the text of the paper, with the corresponding information following later.

Paraphrasing

Paraphrases are an often forgotten but wonderful way of using sources in a research paper. Any time you take quotations from one of your sources and rewrite it into your own words, you are paraphrasing. Many students avoid doing this and prefer instead to use only quotations in their papers, or worse, forget that paraphrases still need citations. Even though paraphrases are written in your own words, you are still using information and ideas originally written by another author, and you must give him or her credit. Otherwise you are still considered to be plagiarizing. Because paraphrases are written in your own words, they should not be surrounded with quotation marks, but they do still need a citation. Remember, you wrote the actual wording; you are just borrowing the ideas, so use the citation to give the author credit without making it seem as though they wrote it.

Tip No. 48 Changing one word does not make something a paraphrase.

A paraphrase should convey the same meaning as the author's original statement but use completely different words. Notice that "words" is plural, which implies a more dramatic rewording than just changing one thing and calling it a paraphrase. Paraphrases allow you to reword another author's statements to add clarity and focus in on the aspects of their writing that relate most specifically to your paper's argument. This is not a blank check to rewrite the author's opinion to make it fit with your argument. Make sure your paraphrases showcase your own writing ability, not your ability to use a thesaurus to vary someone else's word choice.

One of the other great things about paraphrasing is that it will force you to familiarize yourself with more of the subject of the paper. When using a paraphrase, it is key to make sure you change the wording without completely changing the author's original meaning. You do not want to use quotations out of context; similarly, you need to make sure that you do not misinterpret the author's words or ideas when writing a paraphrase. Sometimes it might be tempting to just use a quote rather than look up all of the jargon an author uses in a particularly technical sentence. By using a paraphrase instead, you force yourself to come to a better understanding of the topic. This will make for a better paper because you will be writing with a better grasp of facts and more authority on the subject.

Tip No. 49 **Try using paraphrases rather than quotes in your notes.**

If you have a bad memory or are struggling to get your head around all of the subtle points in your research paper, try forcing yourself to paraphrase while taking notes rather than simply copying down information that seems important. This will force you to engage with the information and create a deeper understanding. You will be more likely to remember the details of what you have read, as well. Even though you are paraphrasing, it is still important to make note of where the paraphrase is coming from for later reference.

When to use a paraphrase

Sometimes it can be difficult to decide when to use a paraphrase instead of a quotation. Looking at a long paragraph full of quotations can be difficult to decipher, especially when the direct quotations are really unnecessary. Sections that have ideas you would like to use are candidates for paraphrases if the author's original wording is not crucial. Sometimes, sentences from a source might only have bits and pieces that apply directly to your topic or might use more jargon and detail than what is needed for your paper. These are great times to use a paraphrase, as well.

Citations and paraphrasing

Paraphrases are a bit trickier to cite than quotations, but not by much. Because paraphrases are not defined by the boundary of quotation marks, telling where a paraphrase starts or finishes can be a bit more difficult. In general, citations for paraphrases can go at the end of the paraphrased sentence or sentences. When referencing specific numbers or statistics within the paraphrase, you might want to include a footnote directly following the number so the reader can check that specific statistic in the source, but this is not a requirement. The citation can also go at the end of the sentence. So long as it is obvious that you are citing the information from the paraphrase, it is not as crucial where the citation goes. It should not matter how long your paraphrase is; as long as the entire thing is coming from the same source, you will only need one citation, so you do not need to worry about including a parenthetical reference or footnote at the end of every sentence in a paraphrase. An exception to this would be if you include a personal aside or explanation that is not taken from the source in the middle of a paraphrase.

Summarizing

Summaries are often confused with paraphrases, but they are subtly different. Summarizing is closer to paraphrasing than quoting but generally covers a wider spread of information than a paraphrase would. Paraphrases usually involve taking a few sentences or a paragraph you might otherwise have quoted and putting it into your own words. Summarizing, on the other hand, gives an overview of key points from several paragraphs, or possibly even an entire chapter or article. The usefulness of summaries will depend greatly on the topic of your research paper and the scope it is meant to cover. If the intended audience is meant to be someone with little or no knowledge of your topic, summaries are a great way to condense relevant ideas and make them manageable.

When using summaries, beware of condensing too much information into a small space. Summaries are great because they allow you to quickly inform the reader of several key points from a much larger piece, but they can be hazardous for these same reasons. Summarizing a large amount of technical information can confuse readers or, at the very least, make them feel inundated. Always try to make summaries easy to follow. It can be tempting to show off your knowledge by trying to use technical or "academic" language geared toward impressing teachers, but keeping things simple is often much better. Using straightforward and simple explanations in a summary gets the point across and proves you know what you are talking about well enough to explain it to people who might not be as familiar with the topic as you. If you are not sure if a summary is out of control, try running it past a friend or roommate to see if they can follow the information.

Tip No.

50 If you cannot decide whether to paraphrase or summarize, remember that summaries condense and paraphrases clarify.

Sometimes, it can be hard to decide whether you are better off using a paraphrase or a summary. In terms of the actual mechanics, there is generally little difference in how to cite each one within your paper, but there is a difference in how you go about writing them. A good rule to follow is that paraphrases are a great way to clarify a piece of information that you otherwise would have quoted, especially in reference to your thesis statement. A summary condenses information for the sake of giving an overview or saving space when an in-depth explanation is not necessary to make your point.

When to use a summary

Whenever you want to condense several pieces of information from multiple places within a source, a summary is your best bet. This is especially true for papers written for a reader unfamiliar with the topic, though they can be useful in other situations, as well. Use summaries to give background information or go over key facts the reader needs to understand to appreciate the technical aspects of your argument. While researching, you will often have to read pages of information just to have a proper understanding of a vital factor that relates to your topic. If readers need to understand something to fully understand or appreciate an aspect of your paper, it is your job as the writer to give them an abridged version. Summaries are often the best way of doing that.

Citations and summarizing

Summaries are usually the most difficult things to cite properly, due largely to the nature of summaries. Not only do they lack the obvious boundaries quotations have, they will often draw on several paragraphs or pages worth of information, unlike paraphrases. They might also use information from more than one source. For these reasons, figuring out where to put citations and what to include in these citations can be confusing and frustrating. To simplify this, use the following guidelines to figure out where to put your citations:

■ If your summary draws from a single source and a single location within that source — such as a page or group of a couple pages within a chapter — you can cite it the same way you would a paraphrase with a single notation or parenthetical reference.

■ If your summary draws from several places throughout the same source — pulling key points from multiple chapters for example — put a citation corresponding to each of these locations next to the piece of information taken from that spot so that the reader can find this information within the source if they choose to look for it, unless you are using a format that does not require you to give page numbers in your citations.

■ If your summary takes information from multiple sources — such as pulling statistics that relate to each other from multiple documents — you must include citations corresponding to each source after the part of the summary taken from that source. Otherwise, the reader will not be able to tell what information came from what source.

This will take a little while to get the hang of, but as long as you look at your citations and continue to ask yourself "Is it clear that this citation corresponds to this information?," you should have no problem placing your citations correctly.

Tip No. 51 Consider investing in a style guide booklet.

Some teachers require you to use a style guide or writer's handbook, but even if your teacher does not, the book is still a worthwhile investment, especially if you are college-bound. The MLA Style Guide is commonly used in both high school and college. Although the tips and tricks in the book you have in front of you will get you started, having a handy desk guide that goes into more depth than this book has the room to do will be useful. Alternately, many web sources have guides to the various styles, so if you are more tech savvy, bookmark a few web guides for later reference.

Using Citations

Citations can be a hassle, but once you learn how, citing sources becomes much less intimidating. Although there are several different methods for citing sources, they all share commonalities that make learning a new citation method easier. This chapter gives you a crash course in the two most common citation methods for research papers. For the sake of illustration, the same fictional sources will be given as samples in each section to highlight the similarities and differences among the styles. Different types of sources are cited differently, so if you need to cite a less common type of source, use a style guide or citation generator to make sure you get the format right. This chapter focuses on citations in your text.

Style Guides: What Are They, and How Are They Used?

A style guide is a handbook that contains the rules and conventions for a particular writing format. Style guides are extremely handy to have on hand because you never know when you are going to run across something new that you will have to figure out how to properly reference. They make troubleshooting while working on citations much easier because they go into more depth than a book about writing papers will.

You can get free access to guides for the major styles online. You might want to bookmark these sites in your Web browser for later reference. If you are the type who likes to have information hard copy, purchase a style manual for whichever style you will be using most frequently. Most major bookstores have entire sections dedicated to writing papers, and they will contain guides for every major writing style plus some more obscure ones. Peruse these, and keep in mind all of the style guides will have similar information. Look for one laid out in a way that is easy for you to navigate. Keep the style guide on your desk for easy reference while writing papers.

Alternately, if you want to have a hard copy but do not have the cash to shell out for a style manual, purchase a cheap binder from a department store and print out excerpts from the online style guides. Put them in the binder, and mark them up with your own notations and reminders. You can always print a new one later.

MLA Format

Many high schools use Modern Language Association (MLA) format as their default paper-writing format. MLA is most commonly used in English classes.

The MLA in-text citation

MLA format uses parenthetical in-text citations. Parenthetical means your citation will be enclosed with parentheses. Inside the parentheses, include the last name of the author and the page number, or numbers, the information being cited was taken from. The author's last name will come first followed by the page number. When citing poetry, use the line number rather than a page number. Do not place a comma between the author's last name and the page number. The citation should also go at the end of the information cited but before the terminal punctuation, a period in most cases. In the cases of particularly short papers or literary analysis not involving any secondary sources, you might only have one location you are drawing information from. In this case, you might use just a page number within the parentheses.

Sample MLA citations

Here is a sample citation. A quote taken from page 15 of John Doe's book *Why Getting Citations Right is Really Important* would be presented as follows:

```
"There is no excuse for getting a citation
wrong," (Doe 15).
```

52 Familiarize yourself with more than one citation method if possible.

You might only need to know the MLA format. However, be aware there are other formats and you may be required to use them, especially if you continue on to college.

APA Format

APA Format is similar to MLA in its origins, but the American Psychological Association authored this style. For this reason, psychology and the social sciences most commonly used this format.

The APA in-text citation

Much like MLA, APA style makes use of parenthetical in-text citations. The biggest difference between a MLA parenthetical reference and an APA parenthetical reference is APA gives the author's last name and the year the piece was published rather than a page number. Unlike MLA, APA also includes a comma between the author's last name and the year.

 53 Pay attention to your commas and periods.

When it comes to citations, the little details make a big difference. It might be hard to believe, but placing a period in the wrong spot or putting a comma in a citation where it does not belong can cost you points. Enough small errors can add up to a lower letter grade, so mind your punctuation.

Sample APA citations

Here is the same sample citation used in the MLA section, but this time it is presented in APA format. The same quote taken from page 15 of John Doe's book *Why Getting Citations Right is Really Important*, published in 2011, would be presented as follows:

```
"There is no excuse for getting a citation
wrong," (Doe, 2011).
```

If you are giving a specific piece of information, you might include a page number in the parenthetical as well. Use your discretion. It would be impossible for this text to cover what to do in every situation, so if you are missing information that would normally be included in the citation, use a style guide to troubleshoot the problem. The APA also has an extensive APA Format Frequently Asked Questions section on their website, which can be found at **www.apastyle.org**.

> Tip No. **54** In-text citations will vary a lot less than bibliographic entries.
>
> Many of these citations look similar, and it might seem there is little difference between citing different types of sources. In the body of the paper, this is true. In some cases, missing information could make these citations different, but for the most part, they are simple. The real differences will become clear when you put together your reference list, bibliography, or works cited page.

Study Guide

❏ Plagiarism is taking the intellectual property of another author and presenting it as your own work.

   ❏ You can still use information from your research in your paper; you just need to give credit to the original author with a citation.

   ❏ Even if you do not think you are presenting someone else's work as your own, it can still be considered plagiarism if it is not cited properly.

❏ Plagiarism is a serious offense in the academic world with real consequences, such as failing and expulsion.

   ❏ Due to copyright laws, you might even face legal action for plagiarism.

❏ You must give credit for every quote, paraphrase, summary, statistic, and other idea you get from another source.

   ❏ When in doubt, use a citation. If you have to ask yourself if something needs a citation, assume the answer is "Yes."

❏ The three most common ways to use research to support your argument are quotations, paraphrases, and summaries.

❏ Quotations insert another author's exact words into your paper.

   ❏ Quotations are best used to highlight information that is worded well and supports your thesis without having to make any changes.

❏ Paraphrases take a specific statement you otherwise might have quoted and put it into your own words.

❏ You may need to use citations and the MLA Style Guide.

CHAPTER 8:
Writing The Introduction

Now that all of the prep work is over, it is time to sit down and actually write the paper. It might seem as if you have spent an exorbitant amount of time planning for the paper, but remember all of the work you have done up to this point will start paying off from here on out. Everything you have done already you would have done anyway, probably while staring at a blank word processor screen feeling frustrated and without any organization or guidance. Now that the guesswork has been taken out, writing an introduction, and then the rest of the paper, will be much more straightforward.

For many people, getting started is the most difficult part. As with citations, writing introductions can be intimidating. Many students are at a loss as to what they should include in an introduction that will properly lead into the paper and still have enough pizzazz to avoid being boring. Some students will even skip writing the introduction when starting their papers and come back to it later. There is nothing inherently wrong with skipping around while writing, but waiting to write the introduction until the last minute can leave you with a poorly written setup to an otherwise great paper. Although this might not completely ruin a paper, it definitely does not do it any favors. The introduction is the first impression readers get of your paper, and if they do not like the look of it, it is unlikely they will want to keep reading. Your teacher will have to read the whole thing, regardless, but your teacher is also far more likely to remember and give high marks to a paper that was impressive from the first lines.

Tip No. **55** Give yourself a filler introduction before jumping into the body of your paper.

If you are really having trouble putting together an introduction that sings, force yourself to at least write a placeholder that sets up your paper. It is okay if this placeholder is not as strong as you would like it to be yet; you can come back later and edit it, but having a brief introduction that sets up the direction of the paper will help you as you write. Just do not forget to go back and fix it up before you turn the paper in!

What to Include

Deciding what to include in an introduction is usually the most intimidating part of trying to write one. A proper introduction draws readers in while providing the setup for the entire paper. Think of putting together your introduction like setting up a row of dominoes. If done correctly, your introduction should set everything up in the reader's mind, as well as in yours, so when it comes time to write the body of the paper, you just have to knock the first one over and watch everything fall into place. A good introduction should do each of the following:

- Hook the reader and pique interest in the topic.

- Provide background information to further draw the reader in.

- Give the reader a general knowledge of what the paper is about.

- Preview key points and lead into the thesis statement.

Some writing instructors or guides might present you with a formula for writing an introduction, and although these can be useful, they can get stale if every single paper you write starts the same way. Moreover, these might not be appropriate for every subject, so rather than give a formula, this chapter will go over what makes a good introduction. There is no single way to write an introduction that will always work for every topic, but these points should act as a good guide.

Writing the hook

The first sentence of the paper is crucial. If you are at all skeptical, think back to all the research you have done. Were there any articles you skipped over after reading only a sentence or two because they did not grab you enough to make you want to use them for your research? If so, you should already realize that by failing to make a paper appealing right from the start, the reader will become disinterested. The same can be said of novels and movies. So, how do you draw a reader in and engage them in your topic?

Tip No. 56   Consider your "ideal reader."

An ideal reader is the hypothetical perfect reader for your paper. Obviously, your teacher will be the one ultimately reading your paper, but depending on the parameters of the assignment, that does not automatically mean your teacher is your ideal reader. You might have been instructed to write the paper as if it were going to be read by someone with no prior knowledge on the subject, or you might be asked to assume your reader is already familiar. Consider these points, and once you know what knowledge level and interests your ideal reader would have, tailor your introduction, and the rest of the paper as well, to meet the needs of this imaginary reader.

Starting with a question or a quotation is a common answer, but these types of hooks have become overused and cliché at this point, so lead into your paper using one of those methods with caution. The best way to find a hook is to compose a sentence that is broad, interesting, and segues nicely into your argument. If the paper opens with a broad or sweeping statement, as opposed to something specifically related to your main point, it will appeal to a wider audience. This will then allow you reel the reader in as you direct their attention to the main point of your paper. If you are having difficulties coming up with something eye-catching enough to grab the reader's attention, consider making a list of what is interesting about your topic. Are there any current events it relates to or controversies associated with it that might be points of interest? Consider who the paper is aimed at informing, and then come up with why that hypothetical reader would be interested in your paper. Devise an opening sentence that would appeal to them.

Using the Inverted Pyramid

Some students might have seen diagrams for how to write a paper that refer to an inverted pyramid. An inverted pyramid, or upside-down triangle, is a good rule of thumb to keep in mind while laying out your introduction. Just as an inverted pyramid is widest at the top and then narrows to a point, your introduction should start out broad and then narrow down to your specific topic and thesis statement. You can vary this formula, especially after you get the hang of writing research papers, but always be sure to narrow down to your thesis statement. Even if you do not start out broad, make sure your introduction complements your thesis statement and leads into it without seeming choppy or forced. It is the main point of your paper, and you have likely spent a lot of time perfecting it, so make sure you have an introduction that allows it to really shine.

Providing background information

Generally, starting out with broad statements to draw readers in can also serve the purpose of informing readers about background topics that relate to the specific issue you are writing about. A proper introduction needs to contain enough background material to allow the reader to understand the thesis statement and what will be argued in the paper. There is no need to go into too much detail at this stage, but giving a brief overview of information pertaining to your research is helpful for the reader. For this reason, introductions are a great place to include summaries. *For more information on summaries, refer back to Chapter 7.*

How much background information is required will depend on the topic at hand. A research paper about a specific historical incident might require more setup than a literary analysis, though there are literary pieces that might require an explanation of the author's motivations or the context in which it was written. There is a fine line you must walk when using background information. Do not give so much that it becomes boring or uninteresting, but include enough so you do not have to spend a lot of time giving background information in the body of your paper. Summarizing in the introduction is usually far more effective. Use your best judgment for how much background information to include. If you are unsure, here are a few questions to ask yourself and help you decide:

Sample Introduction:

> Saturday morning channel surfing
> normally entails bits and pieces of news
> flashing past, as well as flashes of
> color and animated figures being silly to
> entertain millions of kids. Nickelodeon,
> Cartoon Network, and The Disney Channel
> all show cartoons for hours on end. Some
> even play them 24 hours a day. However,
> recently a new type of animation has been
> filtering into televisions all over the
> world. With brightly colored characters,
> insanely huge eyes, and many other
> oddities, they are very different from
> most American made cartoons. "Pokemon,"

"Speed Racer," and "Sailor Moon" are good examples of Japanese anime, which has been slowly making its way into the big time. Anime, Japanese animations, and manga, Japanese comic books, are becoming increasingly popular among American children, teens, and even adults. The Reason? Japanese anime and manga are better than American cartoons.

1. Is there any historical context that is important in understanding this topic?

Take a look at the events that shaped the history of your topic. Perhaps there were significant scientific studies that eventually led to the topic you have chosen. An important court case created the issue your paper tackles, or the time period in which an author was born heavily shaped one of their stories. These are all details you might consider including in an introduction.

For example, the sample introduction included in this chapter might benefit from a historical context. The author could choose to discuss Walt Disney and Osamu Tezuka, two influential figures in animation, rather than needing to explain that later in the paper. Another method might be to give some background on the history of comics and cartoons and how that has led to the development of these cartooning styles.

2. Are there any larger or better-known issues that relate to or lead directly to this topic?

When you did your prewriting, you had to narrow your topic down into something that was easier to grapple with in the space allowed for the assignment. Think back to that larger topic, and ask yourself if there are any better-known issues that are connected to, or perhaps directly led to, the topic you are covering. This is especially useful to consider when writing a paper about a topic that is not widely known. Connecting it to something your readers might know more about will draw them in and help them understand why this topic is important.

For example, if the author of the sample introduction wanted to tap into an issue that has gotten more press, she could discuss the effects of TV and cartoons on child development. This would likely lead to a paper with a different tone.

3. Is there any biographical information that gives a better understanding of this topic?

Depending on the topic, there might be key people involved in it. Authors, scientists, historical figures, or politicians are examples. If any figure or group plays a key role in your topic, consider whether biographical information about the person or group would be useful for the reader. Oftentimes, these details might not be important in the body of the paper, but they make good tidbits to include in an introduction.

As mentioned previously, giving some information about figures such as Walt Disney or Osamu Tezuka in the sample introduction would be an acceptable approach.

4. Are there any statistics or other significant details that would give the reader a better understanding of why this topic is important?

There might be other statistics or ideas that help illustrate why your topic is important and worth reading about. Some of these might have even given you the idea for the paper to begin with. Ultimately, anything that gets the readers' attention and highlights the importance of your topic can become an introduction, so go over your notes again looking for tidbits of information that might work.

For the sample introduction, the author could take a look at the most popular TV shows in American and Japan, for example. A statistic about how many of the most watched TV shows are animated, or are anime imported to America, would grab readers' attention and perhaps give them a different perspective.

5. Does any information fit better later in the paper?

You do not want to use all of the crucial bits of information in your introduction. If your research paper focuses heavily on the biography of a politician or author, it might be unwise to use a lot of biographical information in your introduction. It will steal your thunder later on. Look for bits of information that seem important and lead into your topic but do not necessarily fit in with a later section of the paper. You do not want to weaken your arguments later but rather introduce them using information that will whet the reader's appetite.

6. Can this information be presented in a way that draws readers into this topic?

If the information you are coming up with seems boring or unlikely to grab the reader's attention, play with it a bit and see if there is a way you can word it that makes it catchier or more interesting. The whole point of an introduction is to launch into your topic in a way that makes the reader want to keep reading. If you cannot find a way to do this with the background information you are considering, you are much better off looking for different information to use. Usually, there is a way to make almost anything interesting when presented properly, but it can take significant practice to become adept at that presentation. Experiment with it — you can always scrap an idea and try again.

In the end, how much background information you include is up to you. Practice is the only way to get a feel for how much to include in any given situation because it will vary from topic to topic. Try to make any piece of background information as succinct as possible, and do not be afraid to enlist the help of a writing tutor. They can be great for discussing ideas and will be able to tell you when to include more or less background, among other suggestions.

Tip No. 57 If you are having trouble making up your mind, try writing more than one.

This is not always feasible when you are running on a tight deadline, but if time allows and you are having difficulties deciding how to write your introduction, try writing more than one. If you have two or more ideas, jot them both out quickly and then tuck them away for a few hours before looking them over again. One might stand out more than the other, or you might find you like ideas from both and can mix and match. If you still cannot make up your mind, ask for a second opinion or try looking at them again once you have written more of the paper.

Previewing key points for the rest of paper

The introduction is a lot like the movie trailer for your paper. It should be a preview of what is to come, give enough of an understanding of the key points to interest the audience, but still leave the best for the actual main event. It is always disappointing when you see a movie and all the best parts were already in the trailer. More and more, you will also see trailers for movies that might look cool but really give you no idea as to what the movie is actually about. You want to avoid giving the reader that feeling with your introduction. Your thesis will explain your main argument, but you might want to lead into the thesis by *briefly* bringing up a few of your main supporting details. Give the reader a taste of what is to come, but do not use the most compelling parts of your argument yet. Save those for the body of the paper. Always keep these little previews as concise as possible. This will help you avoid giving away too much in the introduction.

Tip No.

58 An introduction should be all the reader needs to summarize your paper.

A good introduction should allow a reader to tell someone what your paper is about before he or she even reads the rest of the paper. It should not give away all the details but should set up the argument and allow readers to accurately describe it to someone. You can test this by having a friend or parent read your introduction and then tell you what he or she thinks your paper will discuss. If your friend's guess is close to what you had planned on covering, you are doing well. If not, consider some revisions, and ask your friend what parts mislead or confused him or her.

Leading into the thesis statement

Remember that thesis statement you spent so much time on? This is what all that work was for. Your introduction is really just a lead into your thesis, which then leads into the rest of your paper. Take a look at your thesis and what points you bring up in it. Make sure you lead into these points and explain any jargon or concepts mentioned in it that might not be common knowledge. An otherwise great thesis statement can still fall flat if it is not introduced properly. Make sure the sentences leading up to the thesis statement are clearly worded and strong. In addition, double-check to make sure nothing that comes before your thesis statement changes the context of the statement. Consider taking a key word or two from your thesis and including it in the sentence directly before it. Avoid being redundant, but this can help ensure a proper transition from the start of the introduction to the thesis.

Important Note Before Proceeding!

Your paper's thesis statement should already be written at this stage. If it is not, however, it is imperative to write one before continuing with your paper. Without a thesis statement, your paper will lack cohesion and a solid direction. If you have written your thesis already, now is a good time to give it another once-over and make any necessary changes. If you have not edited your thesis at all during the course of your research, chances are it might need a few tweaks now that you are equipped with more information on the subject. For the same reasons you do not want to proceed in writing your paper without a thesis statement, be sure to make sure your thesis has undergone any necessary edits before diving into writing the body of the paper. This is not to say you cannot come back to it later and make further changes, but it will be far easier to make sure everything flows smoothly and logically if your thesis is solid now. *For more details on how to write a thesis statement, see Chapter 4.*

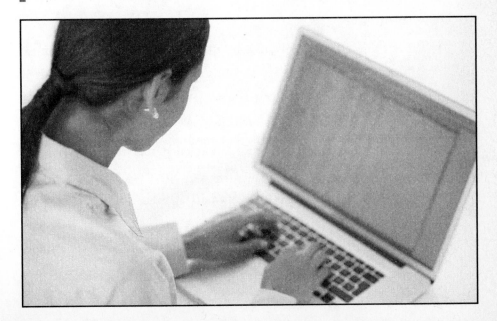

Effective Introduction Techniques

Now that you know what elements make up a great introduction, here are a few techniques you can use if you get stuck trying to figure out where to start. For your convenience, this section will also include a list of things to avoid in your introduction with an explanation of why they should be avoided. Here is your list of Do's and Don'ts for putting together a great introduction:

Do:

- Consider starting with an amusing anecdote or story relating to your topic. These are usually interesting to readers and can give background information on the topic.

- Look for shocking or unusual facts or statistics related to your topic to use in your introduction. Surprising readers is a great way to get them interested and can set up for extrapolation that will lead them into your thesis.

- Think about using humor, if appropriate. Some topics are more somber and would not lend themselves to this technique, but if your topic is more lighthearted, tasteful and witty statements can make great hooks that will interest readers.

- Consider starting with a vividly detailed description of a person, place, or event that is central to your topic. For students with a creative or artistic side, a little dramatization to set the scene for a paper can work well and be fun to write.

Don't:

- Start with a famous quotation, or a quotation in general. It can be tempting to begin with a quotation you found in your research, but you are better off crafting an introduction with your own words.

- Begin with a question. This can be done sparingly, but starting the introduction off with a question has become cliché. If you want to use a question to lead into your introduction instead, try starting with a statement that leads into the question and then asking the question a few sentences into the introduction.

- Use "recipe" metaphors. These statements treat elements of the topic like ingredients in a recipe. They usually read something like "Take a large quantity of X, add Y, and sprinkle with Z, and you get this topic." This format has become gimmicky and cliché.

- Include any other clichés or gimmicks in your introduction. If you are unsure if something is cliché, ask around to see if other people have heard something similar before. Alternately, type phrases into your search engine of choice and see what comes back. If you return a large number of hits, the idea is likely overdone, and you will need to either come up with something more original or find a way to put a new twist on the cliché.

Reinventing the Cliché

You use clichés every single day, whether you realize it or not. Clichés are, by their very nature, overused turns of phrase that have become tired, trite, or boring. These are so ingrained in our language that they will turn up in your writing at some point. Because they are so common, looking for them in your writing can feel like looking for a needle in a haystack. When used sparingly, they are not a deal breaker, but when you go back and reread your writing, take a look for any clichés that might have snuck in. Variety is the spice of life, and clichés are anything but. Clichés are expected, and they will often flow naturally into sentences. If you spot a cliché, be aware of it and consider changing it. Most clichés were, at one point, new and funny. They were so well-liked that they became overused and thus have lost much of their humor and intelligence. It is like beating a dead horse. Try going through your writing and highlighting all the clichés that you find. You will grow a lot as a writer if you try to replace these clichés with new and more inventive phrasing. The removal of the cliché will make the writing better and will likely get your point across more clearly. You can even play with the cliché to show you are aware of it but have chosen to alter it slightly to make it new and fresh. Play around with the words, and see what you come up with and how much better it makes your writing overall.

For example, the phrases "needle in a haystack," "variety is the spice of life," and "beating a dead horse" are all clichés and should be reworded. "Variety is the spice of life" might be reworked to say "diversifying your sentences is more creative as well as more fun." Be creative, get out a thesaurus if needed, and use your own words!

> **Tip No. 59** Use the search engine test to find clichés.
>
> If you are having trouble deciding if something is a cliché, an easy way to tell is to type the phrase into your search engine of choice and see what results are returned. If there are tons of hits with the exact same or similar wording, you probably have a cliché on your hands. If you get few results or results that do not phrase the information the same way as you do in the paper, the chances of it being a cliché decrease.

Sample Introduction

The following is a sample introduction from a paper written about the theme of madness in literature as portrayed in Edgar Allan Poe's short story "The Tell-Tale Heart."

Much of art involved exploring the depths and mysteries of the human mind, from motivations to emotions and even insanity. In fact, many writers seemed to have an intuitive understanding of mental illnesses such as depression, bipolar, and schizophrenia long before they were recognized and defined as conditions. The motif of the descent into madness is one that recurs in art and literature throughout the ages. It can be found in the guilt-torn mind of Shakespeare's Lady Macbeth and the horrors explored in the works of H.P. Lovecraft. Few authors are as famous for writing Gothic tales of madness and horror, however, as Edgar Allan Poe. Many consider Poe to be one of the fathers of the modern Gothic tale, and his reinterpretation of internal horror has influenced countless writers since. Although Poe uses these themes in several of his works, "The Tell-Tale Heart" is a particularly poignant exploration of the personal horror of madness that is even more poignant when viewed in conjunction with modern psychological advances. The narrator assures the reader repeatedly he is not mad, but he is actually trying to convince himself of this, as each instance further illuminates his insanity.

Study Guide

❑ Introductions can seem tricky, but once you know what makes for a great introduction they become quite simple.

❑ A good introduction will do all of the following:

    ❑ Hook the reader and pique interest in the topic.

    ❑ Provide background information to further draw in the reader.

    ❑ Give the reader a general idea of what the paper is about.

    ❑ Preview key points and lead into the thesis statement.

❑ Consider using an anecdote, surprising fact, a dash of humor, or a detailed description to hook the reader.

❑ Take a look at what background information might not fit in with the rest of your paper but might still be good for the reader to know, and consider using it in your introduction.

    ❑ Be sure to include any background information that the reader needs in order to understand your thesis statement.

❑ Think of the introduction like a movie trailer. You want to let the reader know what the paper is about and preview your key points without giving away all the best parts.

❑ Make sure everything in the introduction ultimately leads into the thesis statement and provides the proper context for it.

❑ Remember the inverted pyramid. Start general or broad, and narrow down to your specific thesis statement.

❏ Avoid gimmicks and clichés in the introduction. Your teacher is reading several papers at once, so he or she is well versed in recognizing overused techniques.

CHAPTER 9:
Writing the Body of Your Paper

With your introduction completed, it is now finally time to move on to the heart of your paper. If not all of your prep work paid off while writing your introduction, do not worry. This is where it will really start to make a difference. The body of your paper is everything between the introduction and the conclusion. You have a lot of freedom when it comes to writing the body of your paper, which can be both liberating and frightening. More freedom means more room to experiment and do what you like, but it also means less guidance and more room to make mistakes. There are as many ways to write the body of a paper as there are papers, but even so, here are some basic points to make writing the bulk of your paper easier:

Tip No.

60 Keep all of the work you have done so far handy to keep yourself from getting lost traversing the middle of your paper.

The middle of the paper can be dangerous grounds for the under-prepared. It is easy to lose your point or end up writing in circles while you try to figure out what you want to say. Do not let this happen to you! You are armed with a thesis statement, notecards, and solid outline, so you will have little chance of getting lost. If you see your sentences start to drift off topic, go back to these guides, figure out where you started to diverge from the path, and fix it.

While writing the body of your paper, keep all of the following in mind:

- Make sure your body supports the claims made in your thesis statement.

- Use cited research to support each of your points.

- Explain how the research you are citing supports your argument.

- Develop a rhythm for writing the paper.

- Use your thesis statement and outline in combination to guide your writing.

- Be sure to include transitions between each paragraph in the body.

The rest is ultimately up to you to write, but these tools will help keep you on track and elevate your writing to the next level. To provide additional guidance, the rest of this chapter will be spent examining each of these points in more detail.

Support Thesis Claims

First of all, your body needs to support your thesis statement. Every point you make should go back to your thesis. At each turn, ask yourself "How does this relate to my thesis?" If your body does not adequately support the thesis, the paper has failed. The thesis is your main argument, and you must provide enough evidence to back it up. This point seems obvious, but it is absolutely vital, and you would be surprised by how many students deviate from their theses in the bodies and do not end up sufficiently supporting their original arguments. So, how do you make sure you adequately support your thesis?

Use details for support

As discussed earlier, your thesis statement needs to be argumentative in nature. *For more details on how to accomplish this, see Chapter 4.* Until now, everything you have done has been general in nature. You have been generating ideas, pulling information from sources, forming opinions, and drafting an outline of what you plan to say. What all of that has lacked are details supporting these opinions and ideas. Flesh out these points using specific examples. Expound upon the claims you are making in your thesis. Why do you  believe what your thesis is arguing? What information has led you to form the opinions you have? Look at the points you are planning on covering, and write out the specific details that support these points in relation to your thesis. Take out your notecards, and if you have not already grouped them by topic, do so. Each opinion you plan on presenting in your paper should have one, if not several, specific details associated with it that you are planning on using to support it. Specific details can be anything from examples, to statistics, to data from experiments. The important thing is that you key in on details that show readers why your point is valid rather than simply telling them they should believe what you are saying.

Show vs. Tell:

If you have taken any writing classes or involved yourself in any writing workshops, you have probably heard someone refer to "showing" rather than "telling." Some of your teachers might even have already brought this up. This is commonly addressed in creative writing pursuits, but it is equally applicable to writing academically. Showing is always better than telling, but what exactly does that mean, and why is one better than the other?

Tell - Telling is when you directly tell the reader a fact or opinion and they have to assume that this is true based on that statement.

```
"Chlorophyll absorbs sunlight and
makes grass green."
```

Show - Showing is when you present the reader with descriptions, details, and facts and let them draw conclusions based on that information.

```
"Grass, like most plants, takes
in sunlight to produce essential
nutrients. Chlorophyll absorbs
```

```
sunlight, which triggers a chemical
reaction within the plant to create
the nutrients the plant needs to
survive. Chlorophyll has a greenish
hue, which is why healthy plants are
generally green, and dying or dead
plants are not."
```

Showing can be risky because if you do not present the information properly, your readers might draw different conclusions than you would like them to. It is OK to frame these details and descriptions in a way that guides the reader toward drawing the same conclusions you have and even say directly what your conclusions are, but readers will be better informed and more likely to accept what you are saying if they can see the information that has led you to this conclusion. Showing will also invariably require you to support your points with details, so it is a useful exercise for that reason, as well.

Use cited research

Properly using all the research you have done goes hand-in-hand with supporting your thesis. Most, if not all, of the details you use to support your claims will be taken directly from your notes in the form of statistics, quotes, paraphrases, and summaries. *For more information on the difference between quoting, paraphrasing, and summarizing, see Chapter 7.* Each and every point you make should be backed up by your sources. This lends credibility to your argument and will prevent you from plagiarizing. *More information on plagiarism and its consequences can also be found in Chapter 6.*

Information should be substantiated by credible research

If you have made a quotation outline or you have organized your notecards by topic, then you likely already have a good idea of what support you will be using to back up each of your main points and where this information is coming from. *More information on organizing notecards and quotation outlines can be found in Chapter 6.* Understanding how this research ultimately fits into your paper is key at this stage. Each paragraph of your body should have its own topic or point. In your own words, introduce this idea and explain how it relates to your thesis. Once you have made a connection between this topic and your paper's main point, use examples from your research to substantiate the claims you have made. Drop in details from your notes, and finish by explaining how this detail furthers your argument. This last part will help ensure the reader understands what conclusions to draw from the information and does not confuse your point.

Tip No. **61** **Be kind to your readers, but also be firm.**
Assume your readers are intelligent and do not condescend or talk down to them. Teachers generally do not respond well to students who accidentally take this tone in their papers. Do not confuse treating the reader with respect and being gentle in your argument. Be firm when supporting your thesis without presuming to tell readers what to think. Instead, state facts and show how these facts agree with your argument.

You should also have already checked your sources to make sure that they are credible, but it is possible that as you start to write your paper, you discover there is a hole in your research. You might have a point that you really want to include in your paper, but you cannot find anything to back it up in your other sources. You can go looking for new sources to corroborate your point; just be sure to check these sources the same way you checked the rest of them. It is better to make a different point that might have a little less thunder but that is backed up with credible sources than to add a piece of information at the last minute that turns out to be from a source that is not credible. If your credibility comes into question, even just on one point, readers will have a difficult time believing anything else about your argument. Damaging your credibility can doom an otherwise great research paper. Now is also a great time to double-check the context of all of the information you are using to be sure that you are not misrepresenting any information in order to further your points. *For more information on checking sources for credibility, see Chapter 5.*

Structuring a Paragraph

It may be helpful to think of each paragraph of your paper almost like a miniature paper in and of itself. A good paragraph starts with a topic sentence, which acts as the thesis statement for an individual paragraph. A good topic sentence should focus the paragraph and give the reader an idea of what will be covered in the paragraph. This will also keep your writing focused on supporting the paragraph's main point and keep you from wandering away from your point. Remember, an individual paragraph should contain one well-supported main point. Try to aim for at least three supporting details in each paragraph. You might have more to include, but if you have fewer, your argument might not seem well supported. Of course, this may change depending on the length and scope of the paper, but it is a good general rule.

An outline of a paragraph may look something like this:

1. Topic sentence.
2. First supporting detail
3. Second supporting detail
4. Third supporting detail
5. Concluding/wrap-up sentence with a transition.

If it helps, consider making mini outlines for each of your paragraphs, or use this as a tool to help organize paragraphs that are giving you trouble. Do bear in mind that this outline is an example and is not set in stone. Once you are comfortable writing paragraphs, you may occasionally deviate from these standard guidelines or you may have more or less support for the argument, but this provides a good starting point.

Proper citations included

It is also critical to make sure you cite all of your research properly. Do not wait to put in citations until you are done with the paper, even if it means interrupting your train of thought. If you made notecards or a spreadsheet with all of your notes and citation information, this should not be difficult. If you did not, it is worth taking the time to stop and look up a page number or author as needed. If you wait to do citations until the end, you run the risk of forgetting to come back and finish the citation later. Even if you do not forget about your citations at the end, you might find yourself having trouble finding all of the information you were planning on citing when you go back to it. This is especially true for papers that might be several pages long and need many citations. Quotations are easy to spot, but paraphrases and summaries are not set apart from the rest of the text with quotation marks, so they are more difficult to find at a glance. You might also forget what was a paraphrase or summary when you come back to your paper after a hiatus. This is unacceptable, so take the time and put the citations in as you go. Once you get used to doing citations, they become second nature, so it does not take up any extra time and is worth the effort in the long run.

Tip No. 62 If you cannot put in a full citation at that time, do a partial or use a place marker.

You might run into a situation in which, for whatever reason, you cannot properly cite a piece of information. Perhaps you forgot a book or set of notecards at home or you do not have the time to scour for a page number you forgot to write down. It happens to everyone. When you need to use a reference and you cannot do a proper citation that moment, try to at least put in a partial citation. For MLA format, you can put in parenthesis and the author's name, if you can remember it. If you need to make a footnote, you can start the footnote and make a note there for yourself to come back to it later. Another useful trick is to use your word processor's "highlight" feature to highlight information that does not have a citation yet. This will make it easy to find when you come back to it later.

Develop a Rhythm

This might sound odd, but writing a research paper has a rhythm to it. The more research papers you write, the better you will get at it. This is because the practice helps you establish a rhythm for writing a paper. Even if you are forced to write a paper on a topic you know little about, or in a style that is unfamiliar to you, the rhythm of putting it together should not change much. Having a rhythm will help ensure your information flows neatly from point to point, paragraph to paragraph. You can vary the rhythm, but most paragraphs will follow these steps:

1. Start with a transition and topic sentence that introduces the main point of the paragraph.

2. Add more information to further explain the topic and how it relates to your thesis statement.

3. Back up what you have said so far with information from your sources.

4. Explain how the information you have cited supports your point(s) and adds credibility to your argument.

5. Add additional citations and explanations if you have more for the topic.

6. Repeat until you have covered all of the points you are addressing in the paper.

Tip No. 63 Do not confuse a rhythm with monotony.

Getting into a groove while writing is no excuse to be boring. The best writers know the formats that are most compelling for arguing their points, but they present it in such a way that it is not obvious they are following a formula. Getting a rhythm going will allow you to write faster, but it does not mean you have to format all of your sentences the same way. Do not fall into the trap of laundry listing your points.

There is still plenty of room for variation on this theme, and how you present this information is up to you. You have quite a bit of freedom with your presentation, so choose wording that fits with the type of paper you are writing, as well as the subject matter. You may add lighthearted humor or keep things somber or extremely formal, depending on the class and the topic. Find your voice, and write in a way that is comfortable for you. The basic skeleton underneath all of that will likely stay much the same from paper to paper. For some, this might seem boring, but developing this rhythm will speed up your production speed greatly and also give you a structure to go back to when you get stuck. People who talk about getting into a groove while writing — having the words come easily so they can accomplish a lot in a short amount of time — usually have found a rhythm that allows this.

Tip No. 64 **Your voice is where you are allowed to be creative, but make sure your tone matches the topic you are covering.**

Many writers will talk about developing a style or "voice." If you have a favorite author, you might be able to recognize his or her work just by reading a bit of it, even without seeing the byline. This is because that author has developed a unique style that is easily recognizable. The more you write, the more you will find your own voice. Your voice usually is dictated in part by your personality. It might be easy-going, formal, witty, or comedic. Although using a voice will make your paper uniquely "you" and allow you to be a little creative, be sure that developing your voice and inserting some personality into your writing does not clash with the topic you are covering. Somber topics might not be suited to a humorous tone, and some classes might require a formal tone. You can still be creative; just make sure that it does not interfere with properly covering the topic at hand.

Follow Outline and Thesis Statement

Your outline and thesis statement are your guides for writing your paper, so refer back to them often. This will keep you on track and ensure you do not deviate from your points. Without an outline, writers often find themselves meandering away from their main points while they try to figure out what it is they want to say. Having an outline means you should never have to ask yourself "What comes next?" You should be able to look at your outline and have your answer. No matter what kind of outline you made, your main points should be listed out in some fashion. Whenever you slow down or find yourself at a loss as to what comes next, find the next point on your outline and start writing about it.

Tip No.

65 Look to your outline to craft your topic sentences.

Depending on the type of outline you made and how much work you put into it, you likely have the basis for some, if not all, of the topic sentences you need for your paper already started. Remember that a topic sentence is a mini-thesis statement and should tell the readers what will be covered in the paragraph they are about to read. When you start a new paragraph, your outline should be the first place you look. Once you have the paragraph's topic sentence written, the rest of the paragraph should flow easily.

Refer back to your thesis statement often. Each paragraph should address something related to your thesis. Having it handy will ideally help you avoid getting stuck while addressing that part of each paragraph. Your outline will likely contain the start to many, if not all, of the topic sentences for each paragraph of your paper. You can then add details and clarification to these ideas and pull up the research you will be using to support these points. If you are unsure what research to have ready for the next part of your paper, refer to your outline. Referring back to an outline also makes it much easier to develop the rhythm discussed in the previous section. You already know what is coming next, so keep that in mind as you write, which will help you create transitions and ensure that your paragraphs flow together.

Tip No.

66 Print out or write down your thesis statement and outline for easy reference.

These days, many students do almost everything digitally. If your outline is digital and your thesis statement is embedded in your introduction, you will likely have to toggle between windows on your computer to see your outline or scroll up to your thesis. This can be a pain and it makes it difficult, if not impossible, to compare them side-by-side. To save yourself some hassle, print out your outline or take a few moments to jot it down in a notebook. You might want to consider writing your thesis statement down on a notecard or Post-it® note and keeping it somewhere visible on your desk or even on the corner of your computer monitor.

Coherency is also a big concern with research papers. Papers that lack coherency are easy to spot because they jump from point to point and often leave the reader feeling confused. Following your outline will make sure your paper does not feel disjointed. This is not to say you cannot make any changes to your outline at all. You might find as you are writing that switching the order of your paragraphs makes for a stronger argument or a clearer logical progression from one idea to the next. If that situation comes up, feel free to make the changes. The important thing is to make sure you still cover all of your points and that changing the outline makes your paper easier to follow. Whenever you reorder paragraphs, or even sentences within paragraphs, make sure you reread them for coherency. Make any changes necessary to accommodate the change, be it adding a new transition or changing the wording to make it less confusing in the new context. Transitions will be covered more thoroughly in the next section.

Must flow neatly from one topic to the next

Transitions are an important but often forgotten topic. Good transitions between paragraphs are another small set of details that separate an OK research paper from a great one. So, what exactly is a transition, and how do you use it effectively? Transitions are words and phrases that help a paragraph flow into the paragraph that follows it. Good transitions let the reader know the paper is changing to another point without catching him or her off guard. Transitions can be subtle or direct, but

if they are absent entirely, your paper will feel choppy and disorganized. Transitions add coherency to the body of your paper and will make it much easier to read.

Direct transitions rely on a transitional word or phrase to signal to the reader that the topic is changing and usually give some clue as to the relationship between the point of this paragraph and the one that preceded it. Words such as "nevertheless," "additionally," "similarly," "first," "last," and "furthermore" are direct transitions. Transitional phrases can be used as well, such as "on the other hand," or "despite the fact that," among others.

The following is an example of a direct transition taken from an analysis of Freud's research on Coca:

```
...He also devotes time to discussing
other medical uses of coca, such as
```

treating stomach problems, long-term use
for diseases that involve the degeneration
of tissue, treatment of morphine and
alcohol addiction, the treatment of
asthma, use as an aphrodisiac, and use as
a local anesthesia.

On the one hand, he does cite the use of
coca as experienced by several different
people, which is good because it helps
eliminate the possibility of different
people having widely varying reactions to
the drug. He experiments with different
potencies of his solution and explains
that different doses have different
effects on different people based on
their tolerance...

The words "on the one hand" transition the reader from the list of things that Freud discusses at the end of the first paragraph to the analysis of his actual experiments. A phrase such as "on the one hand" is generally followed by a contrasting "on the other hand" point.

Subtle transitions also link the new paragraph to the one before it, but they do it indirectly. To write a subtle transition, take a few key words from the last sentence of the paragraph before the transition and work them into the opening sentence of the new paragraph. This creates a link between the information in the readers mind and shifts to a new point without feeling abrupt or creating confusion.

The following is an example of a subtle or indirect transition taken from a paper about morality in epic literature:

```
Funeral rights and being able to have
a proper hero's burial for warriors who
died in battle is an important cultural
value, as shown through Beowulf's grand
funeral at the end of the epic. Grendel
devours his victims, so this is not even
an option. He is an instrument of death
and destruction, which shows that these
more physical concerns are the major
manifestations of evil in the world
of Beowulf.

    The portrayal of evil in Beowulf is
fairly straight forward, leaving little
question as to what is and is not evil.
Evil also does not masquerade as anything
else, which is a large difference between
the villains in Beowulf and the villains
in Spencer's The Faerie Queene.
```

Notice how the last sentence of the first paragraph contains the words evil and *Beowulf*. The beginning of the next chapter also uses both of these words, but changes the focus from the manifestations of evil in *Beowulf* to the straightforward nature of this evil in comparison to *The Faerie Queene*. The topic changes, but by using points brought up at the end of the previous paragraph to start the next one, the train of thought flows smoothly from one topic to the next.

Both transition techniques are effective, and some paragraphs might lend themselves better to one or the other. The best papers will use a mix of both. In the end, do what feels right. As long as the paragraphs flow together neatly, your transitions are working. If you have any doubts about your transitions, try reading the paper aloud and see if you stumble between ideas. Alternately, try having a friend or parent look it over and get a second opinion.

CASE STUDY: ADVICE FROM A COLLEGE PREP TEACHER

Patrick Davey
Teacher
Lane Tech College Preparatory School
http://DaveyBio.yolasite.com

I have written a plethora of papers for all disciplines during my education at my high school and university, ranging from data-driven lab reports to poetry analysis. I also grade primarily college-level writing for my career as a college preparatory teacher.

Having great resources really separates a great paper from a so-so paper. Remember that Wikipedia is not generally held as a credible source, but the links used as references in the articles can be. Always cross reference your information, as well. The problem with anyone being able to write anything is that they do.

Being able to be fluent in your writing and provide a lot of meaningful exposition is beneficial, but by itself can produce only a paper of fluff. Well-respected and relevant resources provide a necessary backbone to papers written at this level. Remember that in a research paper, you are not telling a person about a topic, you are explaining your argument to the reader. Keep asking yourself "Why?" By answering this question over and over, you'll break down the topics so you do not leave the reader with any questions. Make sure your support ties to your thesis, and list out where different sources you have available to you would fit best. The rest of writing the paper is just making connections.

Do not value another person's writing over your own. People value different styles, and it plays to the individual. Be original in your writing, and your teachers will see your true skill and be able to give back the most effective feedback tailored specifically to you.

If you are having issues, try taking a seminar or reading a book on crafting papers. Expose yourself to well-written high school and college-level papers so you know what to expect, and take advantage of the fact that many papers at this level come with an objective rubric. Use it as a checklist to ensure a good grade.

Tip No. 67 Set goals based on output, not time.

It is no secret that high school students are busy. Finding time to sit down and write a paper between classes and extracurriculars can be difficult, if not impossible. Although it might be tempting to make plans to sit down and work on a paper for an hour and then do something else, this often leads to procrastination and a lot of time spent messing around until that hour is over. To increase productivity, try setting goals such as "I will write 500 words before practice" or "I will write two pages before I go to bed."

Study Guide

❏ The body of your paper consists of everything between your introduction and your conclusion. It is the largest part of your paper.

❏ The entire point of the body is to support the claims made in your thesis statement, so keep asking yourself "How does this relate to my thesis?"

❏ Use cited research to support each of your main points.

    ❏ Do not skip putting in citations or put it off until later. This will increase the chances that you will forget a citation.

    ❏ If you absolutely have to skip adding a citation, make a notation that is easy to spot so you can find it again later.

❏ Follow every citation with an explanation of how this information supports or furthers your argument.

❏ You have a lot of room for experimentation with the body, but try to find a rhythm of citations and explanations.

    ❏ Do not confuse getting a rhythm going with being boring or repetitive.

❏ Your thesis statement and outline should both act as a map for writing.

    ❏ If you get lost or find yourself asking "What do I write next?" refer back to your thesis statement and outline.

    ❏ Keep a copy of each handy so you can refer back to them as often as you need.

❏ When possible, remember to "show" readers rather than simply "tell" them information.

❑ Include transitions between every paragraph in your paper so it flows together neatly.

    ❑ Transitions can be direct or indirect.

    ❑ Vary your transitions to avoid becoming repetitive.

    ❑ Use a few key words from the last sentence of a paragraph in the topic sentence of the next paragraph to link them together.

CHAPTER 10

Wrapping Things Up, The Conclusion

By this point, you should have finished your introduction, as well as the body of your paper. The end is now in sight, which can be both exciting and draining. It can be tempting at this point, especially if you are looking at a looming deadline, to quick slap a few sentences that seem to wrap things up and call it good enough. Experienced and inexperienced writers alike can run into this problem, especially after long marathon writing sessions. Fatigue sets in. Do not give in to the temptation to throw something together and call it "good enough." You have spent a considerable amount of time and effort on this project so far, so why potentially throw it all away now with a ramshackle conclusion?

The conclusion is the last thing your reader will see, so it should be memorable. A poor conclusion will leave readers feeling unsatisfied or as if they have wasted their time. Even if the rest of the paper was great, people remember the conclusion and will make judgments based on that. If you have ever watched a movie or read a book and been truly absorbed by it but were disappointed by the ending, then you should already know this. You likely walked away from the book or movie remembering what you did not like about the end rather than the parts that were enjoyable. No one wants readers to finish reading their work and be left thinking "What was the point?" or "Why did I even bother with this?" For this reason, you need to make sure that you give yourself enough time to properly write and edit a conclusion that complements the rest of your paper.

Tip No. **68** Trick yourself into allowing extra time to write your conclusion.

If you tend to procrastinate or budget all of your time for writing the main body of your paper and run out of time for the conclusion, try tricking yourself into thinking you have less time than you actually do. Give yourself one deadline for everything up until the conclusion, take a break, then come back and give yourself an extra chunk of time to write the conclusion. If possible, try to get everything else done a day early so you can spend the last day before your deadline on the conclusion and editing.

Writing a good conclusion is simple, but it is not always easy. This might seem contrary, but remember that there are quite a few things that sound simple but require some effort. Climbing a rock-wall, for example, is not that difficult to explain, but it does require a lot of effort to actually complete. A good conclusion will review the key points of the paper as well as explain to the reader why the information is important, relevant, applicable, or how it relates to the world as a whole. Although this does not sound complicated, many students balk at writing a conclusion, or worse, ignore it until the last minute and then do not put any time or effort into it. Succumbing to common pitfalls or rushing through a conclusion to meet a deadline can sour an otherwise great paper. The rest of this chapter will examine what makes a good conclusion, as well as what to avoid while writing your conclusion.

Effective Conclusion Techniques

One of the easiest ways to write a great conclusion is to take the same formula you used for your introduction and then reverse it. Where introductions use an inverted pyramid structure, conclusions generally use a pyramid structure. Rather than start out with broad statements and then narrow down to the thesis statement, a conclusion should do all of the following (generally in this order):

1. Restate the thesis.

2. Reiterate the key points of the paper.

3. Explain why the paper is relevant in the broad sense or what the reader should take away from the paper.

Conclusions: Pyramid Structure

If you read the Inverted Pyramid sidebar found in Chapter 8, then this should look somewhat familiar. Use this thought process as a guide while writing your conclusion, much like you did with your introduction. This time, the pyramid is right-side up. The principle is the same, but the execution will be different. Your conclusion should start with a narrow statement that transitions the reader from the previous paragraph to the paper's main point. Once this main point has been reestablished, additional details should be added to remind the reader of what they have read. Guide the reader from the specific focus of your paper to the broader considerations, such as how this research fits into a discipline, area of study, or the world as a whole.

Do not forget:

Conclusions are written like Pyramids.

Introductions are written like Inverted Pyramids.

Do not get them confused! If it helps, draw yourself a diagram:

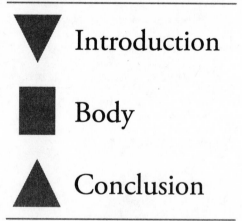

If you are a visual learner, remember that the diagram resembles a wrapped piece of candy.

Restate the thesis

Restating the thesis is along the same lines as reviewing the key points of the paper, but it deserves its own section because many students have trouble with it. The best way to start a conclusion is by restating the thesis of your paper. Keep in mind that restating is not the same thing as repeating, so do not just copy and paste the thesis straight from the introduction. Although you certainly can start there, you need to change the structure and wording. This will keep you from sounded repetitive as well as show your mastery of the topic.

> **Tip No.**
> **69** **Avoid sounding apologetic.**
> A common mistake made in conclusions is using phrases such as "I am not an expert, but..." or "This paper has tried to show..." Using these phrases makes it sound as though you are apologizing to the reader for flaws and inadequacies in your paper. This is never OK. You need to leave the reader feeling satisfied, as if he or she learned something by reading your paper. Be firm in your conclusion, just as you were in the introduction.

The restated thesis should address all the same points as the thesis but also have an air of finality. Remember, you are not telling the reader what you are going to attempt to prove this time; you are telling them what you have proven through the research presented in the paper. The first step in doing this is taking a look at your thesis statement and rewording it to remove any references to what will be discussed. Everything has already been discussed, so the tense should reflect this. Once you make sure the tense is appropriate, try varying your word choice a bit so it hits on the same major points but is different enough that it sounds fresh.

Review or reiterate key points

> **Tip No. 70** Dig up rough drafts and notes to get inspiration for your conclusion.
>
> Odds are good that if you have done everything suggested in this book, you have rough drafts of thesis statements, topic sentences, and outlines. Consider keeping these documents in a folder, either digitally or in hard copy, so you can go over them later. Wording that you scrapped the first time around can sometimes be polished and make for a great conclusion.

With the start of the conclusion out of the way, the next step is to review the main points from the paper. To start, look back at the body of your paper, or refer to your outline. Make note of the topic sentence of each of your paragraphs. Much of the time, you can reword these sentences the same way you reworded your thesis statement and then incorporate that into the introduction. This will quickly summarize the important details and keep you from spending too much time summarizing. Particularly striking quotations or statistics can also be repeated here, but try not to use more than one or two. The conclusion represents your closing thoughts on the topic, so it should primarily consist of your own words.

On top of summarization and quotations, conclusions may also contain recommendations to the reader or relevant questions that further the thesis. Ask yourself what you would ideally like to see readers do in reaction to your paper. Is there an action they should take or something they should examine or investigate further? Is there a bigger issue that your research draws attention to? Your reader will want to know the answer to these questions, so take a moment to reflect on what your ideal end results would be. For example, a paper on energy conservation might encourage readers to add eco-friendly practices to their lives. A research paper on a political proposal might ask readers to write to congress and voice their opinion.

Tip No. 71

Create unity and wholeness in your paper by referencing your introduction in your conclusion.

By restating your thesis in your conclusion, you are already starting to achieve a sense of unity in the paper. Look and see if there are other key words, phrases, or ideas that are mentioned in your introduction that fit into your conclusion. These can be subtle, but connecting the introduction to the conclusion in this way will help leave readers feeling satisfied. This is what it means to have your paper or argument come full circle.

Provide resolution

Although it is okay to encourage readers to question their opinions or introspect on the bigger picture your topic is a part of, this is not an excuse to leave loose ends. You need to provide a sense of resolution, so make sure your conclusion wraps up your argument. Consider rereading the body of your paper and making a note of any details you feel should be touched on in the conclusion to make the paper feel complete. You also can keep a running list of these details while you write. Do not underestimate readers or assume they will not notice one or two forgotten details. Even if they cannot explain exactly what is missing, readers will feel somehow unsatisfied with a paper that does not provide resolution.

Tip No.

72 End your conclusion with something memorable, such as a question, warning, or call to action.

The conclusion of your paper needs to address one important question the reader will likely have: "Why should I care?" Ending your conclusion with a broad question that causes readers to consider how to use the information they have learned is one way of resolving this. Depending on the topic, ending with a warning or a call to action are also great options. By warning the reader of something that might come about if people do not take notice of the issue you are covering, or by asking the reader to step up and do something to change a situation, you have given them a reason to care as well as a possible way to use the information contained in your paper.

Traps to Avoid

Now that you understand what makes a good conclusion, it is important to understand what common mistakes students make while writing conclusions. Even if your conclusion meets all of the criteria listed previously, there are errors that will weaken or outright ruin a conclusion. The following sections will explain some of the most common traps students fall into and how to avoid them.

Over summarization

Although summarization is a key part of any conclusion, it is important to remember that it is not the only thing a conclusion consists of. Many students make the mistake of simply rehashing what they already stated in their papers and then trailing off. These conclusions are weak because they do not leave the reader with a sense of resolution. Summarization is necessary to remind the reader of what the main points are, but this alone does not give readers a sense of what to take from the paper. Explaining how to apply the information covered in the paper is just as important as refreshing the reader on all of the key points. Try to keep summarization to no more than half of your conclusion.

If you find yourself relying on too many summarizations, try looking to see if you can make any of these statements more concise without losing any important details. Once you have whittled your summarization as much as possible, try making a list of reasons why you believe your paper is important. Look at these points, and see if any of them can translate into questions or statements to pose to the reader.

Introduction of new information

Another common mistake students make is introducing new information in their conclusion. It is easy to do accidentally, especially when giving the reader a sense of how the information in the paper applies to the world at large. It is OK to pose questions or explain how the information is relevant, but do not introduce key points that were not previously addressed in the paper. If you find yourself introducing new information at this stage in the writing process, stop and ask yourself why this information was not included earlier in the paper. If it seems important, then go back to your body and add the information there. If it is not important enough to earn a mention in the body of the paper, then it does not deserve to be included in the conclusion.

Tip No. **73** Do not use your conclusion to try to make up for inadequacies in the body of the paper.

Sometimes, when you find you have not covered all of the information in your paper that you originally intended to, the temptation is to throw whatever you missed into the conclusion. These conclusions are problematic because they do not actually conclude anything. They do not wrap up a paper; they only introduce more questions. This often happens when students do not narrow their topics enough. If you find you have information that has not been covered by the end of the paper, consider readdressing the scope of the paper to something narrower.

If you find you have a bunch of information that was meant to be included in the paper but that was left out for whatever reason, this might be a sign that the topic you chose is too broad. Look at the information you are trying to introduce into the conclusion, and see if there is any sort of pattern or common theme. If so, take a look at your thesis and see if you can rework it so this extra information is not necessary. An excess of unused information might also indicate a lack of focus, so reread your paper for cohesion. If you are not sure what, if anything, to leave out, try asking a tutor for help.

Sample Conclusion

The following is a sample conclusion from a paper about Neopagan religions and how they are adapting to modern technology:

```
Many modern Pagan practices are quite
different from what is believed to be
the traditions of ancient pre-Christian
religions, but there are still
```

similarities. Several of the differences
that some modern Pagans embrace have been
adapted from these ancient practices to
make them more applicable to the modern
world. The emphasis on individualism
within the various Pagan traditions
lends itself to adaptability, which is
one of the numerous reasons Paganism is
still surviving in modern cities and
urban environments. Many Pagan practices
are also similar to other major, or
more mainstream, world religions. This,
combined with the fact that so many people
are familiar with the lore surrounding
the ancient pantheons of gods, makes
converting to Paganism easy for those
who desire to. Although it remains true
that many ancient Pagan practices are not
completely compatible with the modern
world, the creative and devout still find
ways to commune with nature in local parks
and draw energy from power lines and water
pipes. The Neopagan movement is evolving
into a religion with the capacity to
thrive in a fast paced, technologically
driven, urban world, possibly even more so
than several mainstream religions.

CASE STUDY: GREAT CONCLUSIONS MAKE FOR GREAT PAPERS

Matt Sias
Student
University of Wisconsin - Eau Claire

I wrote and edited many psychology-related research papers in college. I also did a great deal of writing and editing technical documents and step-by-step instructional documentation. I was an editor on my high school newspaper and wrote a lot for class in high school. Additionally, I have experience writing and editing public policy and financial legislation. Beyond that, I have studied, and frequently exercised, written interpersonal communication.

Great papers tend to have interesting and thoughtful introductions and conclusions. Often, not-so-good papers will only include an introduction and conclusion out of necessity, and they really add nothing to the overall worth of the paper. Great papers also have a logical progression and smooth transitions. It is easy to tell if the author has reviewed the order of topics. Transitions are really the key to helping the reader understand the author's ideas and, therefore, must aid the reader in moving from one topic to the next.

Leverage library employees to help with research and interpret the meaning of any findings. Put your pen to paper, and write a rough draft. Ask your peers, instructor, and other resources to critique it. Spend time polishing the paper; you might go through many drafts. If you feel stuck, ask for help!

A good thesis statement outlines main points very clearly and often takes a stance on the topic of the paper. Do not leave the readers guessing what will be covered.

Make the reader care about your topic. You do not need to write a "speech-style" introduction with a shocking statistic or rhetorical question. Write to your audience. This can be accomplished through the previously mentioned methods, but it can also be accomplished by simply making your topic relevant to the reader.

Great conclusions revisit the main topics in a way that is unique and different from the rest of the paper. Do not simply list the things that were discussed. Do not introduce any new facts or information in a conclusion that was not mentioned earlier in the paper. Calls to action or thought-provoking statements make for a strong finish.

Study Guide

❏ Be sure to leave yourself enough time to write a proper conclusion. Tacking on a few sentences at the end of your paper is not acceptable.

❏ A good conclusion will do all of the following:

    ❏ Restate the thesis.

    ❏ Summarize the paper's main points.

    ❏ Explain how the topic fits into the big picture or what the reader should take away from your research.

❏ The most common way to start a conclusion is by restating the thesis. Remember, restating does not mean repeating.

❏ Look to your topic sentences and outline to gather the main points the conclusion should review.

    ❏ If you have rough copies of topic sentences or thesis statements, take them out and look them over to get ideas for your conclusion.

❏ Ask yourself what you would like the reader to do after reading your paper. If there is a point you want them to consider or an action you want them to take, make that obvious in the conclusion.

❏ The conclusion should be written in pyramid structure, the opposite of the structure used in introductions.

❏ Try to incorporate words and ideas from your introduction into the conclusion to show that the paper has come full circle.

❏ Avoid these common traps:

  ❏ Do not over summarize or rely on summary alone in your conclusion.

  ❏ Do not introduce new information in the conclusion.

  ❏ Do not attempt to make up for inadequacies in the conclusion; go back and fix the problem in the rest of the paper.

CHAPTER 11:

Formatting and Reference Pages

With the conclusion out of the way, it is time to put the finishing touches on the research paper before proofreading and editing. In the hustle and bustle of finishing a major project, it can be easy to neglect or entirely forget about details such as formatting, but making sure the paper is formatted correctly is important and should not be forgotten. You also need to allow yourself enough time to compile your reference page. Do not make the mistake of thinking you can ignore your reference page until the last minute. Reference pages can be time consuming, so allowing yourself enough time to make sure your references are compiled correctly is vital.

There are countless ways to format a paper. The same can be said for reference pages. Each type of source has unique rules for proper inclusion in a reference page. Entire books have been dedicated to understanding formatting and citations for the various writing styles. These are known as style guides, and it is highly recommended that you invest in one. It is not possible to adequately address every aspect of this topic in one chapter, so instead this chapter will give you a basic understanding as well as show you what tools are available to make this step of the writing process easier.

Formatting the Paper

The words "proper formatting" have been mentioned several times so far, but what does this really mean? Formatting refers to the general layout and appearance of a written document, in this case your paper. This includes the font, font size, spacing, alignment, margins, headers, footers, and more. MLA, APA, and Chicago Style all have unique requirements when it comes to formatting. Your teacher may impose additional requirements based on personal preferences.

Tip No. **74** **Remember that formatting is part of the editing process.** It can be easy to forget that the formatting of your paper is something you will likely be graded on. For this reason, be sure to double-check your margins, fonts, headings, charts, and diagrams to make sure they are consistent and uniform and they look good on the page. Most teachers or writing styles have requirements for margins and fonts sizes, so make sure you check these details before calling it "done."

Finding formatting requirements

The first step in ensuring that a paper is properly formatted should be checking your assignment sheet or class syllabus for any instructions. Most teachers will include what font, size, spacing, and margin sizes they prefer, as well as any other details. In some cases, they might just require the paper be written in standard MLA, APA, or Chicago format. If this is the case, check a style guide — either online or in hard copy if you have one — for this information.

How to adjust the format

Your word processor should be equipped with all of the tools you need to properly format your paper. If you do not have access to Microsoft Word or a similar program on your computer, consider downloading a free one, such as OpenOffice. OpenOffice can be downloaded from **www. openoffice.org**. Thankfully, no matter what program you use, the majority of the menus are standardized and will be the same or similar from program to program. Do keep in mind, however, that by using a program like this, you might run into formatting issues when you transfer the document from OpenOffice to Word and vice versa. You should also double-check your file extensions to make sure you are saving in a format that can be read by multiple programs, such as .doc.

The tool bars at the top of your word processing screen will be all you need to complete basic formatting tasks. When changing the format of text that is already written, be sure to highlight or select all of the text you are altering. Once the text is selected, you can change the font and font size using the drop down menus at the top of the page, or along the ribbon, in newer versions of Microsoft Word, as well as adjust the typeface to bold, italicized, or underlined. You can also use the alignment buttons to center information on the page.

The Format drop down menu or button is also used to adjust the line spacing and margins. To change the line spacing, open the "Paragraph" menu. Under the "Indents and Spacing" menu there should be a drop down menu called "Line Spacing." Use this to change from single to double spacing. Likewise, the "Page" menu, also found under the Format menu, will allow you to change the margin width on the top, bottom, left, and right sides of the page. If you cannot find these menus in your word processor, use the program's help feature to find where these tools are located.

The majority of papers you write will be written in Times New Roman, 12 point font, double spaced, and aligned left, so consider making these the default in your word processor to save some time.

Headers and footers

Sometimes you will be required to include a header or footer in your paper with certain information in it. These are sections at the top or bottom of each page of the paper and usually include information such as the author's name, the page number, or the title of the work. Inserting these into your document is simple. The "View" drop down menu at the top of the screen should have an option for both headers and footers. If not, reference your programs help menu.

One thing to note, however, is that headers and footers will contain the exact same information on each and every page of the document. This means that if you need to put a page number in the header or the footer, you cannot simply type the number in on each page. Instead, you can insert what is called a "field." This option is located under the Insert menu, and there will likely be options to insert the page number, date, time, etc. If you cannot find this feature, check the help menu for information on how to do this in your program.

> ## Tip No. 75 Give the paper a once over while holding it upside-down.
> This tip is especially important for papers that include visuals, such as charts, graphs, or pictures. Looking at the paper upside down will make it easier to spot formatting or placement issues, such as incorrect font sizes, poor spacing, and margin errors. It is also usually easier to tell if something is off center if you look at it upside down as well as right side up.

Reference Pages

Reference pages are easily one of the most complicated parts of writing a research paper. Each style has a different way of including information in the reference page. They also call the reference page by different names. Each different type of source, including books, magazines, websites, and interviews, has a different format and different information that will need to be included in the entry. For this reason, either obtaining a copy of the style guide for whichever style you will be using most frequently or making use of free online style guides is extremely important. Regardless of how daunting or frustrating putting together a reference page might seem, it must be included in every research paper.

> ## Tip No. 76 Always include as much information as possible on your sources.
> Long-form citations call for all sorts of details about the source. These vary widely depending on the type of source, but you likely will find yourself in a situation in which a citation asks for more information than you have available on the source. Your source might not have obvious pagination, or you might be missing a publication location, for example. In this case, it is acceptable to leave this information out of the citation. But do not use this as an excuse to be lazy with your citations. Always be sure to include as much information as you can.

What is a reference page?

A reference page, also called a works cited page or bibliography, is a detailed list of all the sources used in a research paper. This is generally the last page in any paper. The reference page should contain enough information that the reader can find the exact source you used.

The importance of reference pages

Even if you provide an in-text citation for every piece of information you include, your citations will not be complete unless they lead the reader to a matching entry on the reference page. If you do not provide a reference page or your reference page is not done properly, you might find yourself in trouble for plagiarism or falsifying information.

Rather than give a list of all of the hundreds of types of citations, the rest of this chapter will instead provide information on where to go to find the format for citations in MLA and APA, and offer an example of what a reference page in each style might look like.

Tip No. 77 Make a list of all sources cited in your paper, and compare that with your bibliography.

Depending on the format of your in-text citations, this can be tricky. Parenthetical citations are easier to spot than footnotes. Nonetheless, double-check your in-text citations to make sure they are included in your bibliography or works cited page. This is especially important for long research papers that require a a lot of sources. It can be easy for one to slip through the cracks, so keep a list handy of all the sources you used so you can cross-reference that with your bibliography.

MLA Works Cited

A reference page in MLA style is called a works cited page. This page will have the title "Works Cited" centered at the top. It will then list all the sources you have cited in alphabetical order. If the citation takes up more than one line, indent all other parts of the citation. Information for MLA citations can be found in detail at **www.mla.org**.

Sample

Works Cited

Archer, Shirley. "For Heart Rate, Tai Chi Comparable to Brisk Walk." IDEA Fitness Journal 5.3 (March 2008): 78(1). Academic OneFile. Gale. Carthage College/WAICU. 23 Apr. 2008 <http://find.galegroup.com/itx/start.do?prodId=AONE>.

Hardy, Annabel, Alice Solomon, and "Ki Treatment: Healing with Sound and Touch." Positive Health Magazine 142(2007):

Allen, Mark. "Tai Chi Do." Tai Chi Do. 25 Apr 2008 <http://www.taichido.com/chi/home.htm>.

Tip No.

78 Double-check all your citation punctuation.

Misplaced periods and commas are not worth losing points over. Though the details vary depending on which format your paper is in, most citation requirements have strict punctuation guidelines. It might seem silly or unimportant, but every little punctuation mark counts.

APA Reference Page

A reference page in APA style is called a Reference Page. This page will have the title "References" centered at the top. It will then list all the sources you have cited in alphabetical order. Though the format of the individual citations will be different, the presentation is identical to MLA style. Information for APA citations can be found in detail at **www.apa.org**, or on the Purdue OWL at **http://owl.english.purdue.edu**.

Sample

<u>References</u>

Archer, S. (2008). "For heart rate, tai chi comparable to brisk walk". *IDEA Fitness Journal, 78*(1), Retrieved from **http://find.galegroup.com/itx/start. do?prodId=AONE**

Hardy, A., & Solomon, A. (2007). Ki treatment: healing with sound and touch. *Positive Health Magazine, 142.*

National Center for Complementary and
    Alternative Medicine, (2008). *Tai chi*
    for health purposes National Center for
    Complementary and Alternative Medicine.
    Retrieved from **http://nccam.nih.gov/**
    health/taichi

Tai chi: improved stress reduction,
    balance, agility for all. (2008).
    Retrieved from **http://www.mayoclinic.**
    com/health/tai-chi/SA00087

Tip No. 79 Double-check the order of sources in your bibliography.

Depending on the assignment, you might be asked to divide your sources up by type or topic, but this is rare. Most commonly, sources are listed in alphabetical order within the bibliography. Make sure you have ordered your sources properly. Failing to do this will make your bibliography more difficult to navigate for you and the reader.

Tip No. 80 Be consistent.

Do not get creative with fonts, margins, and sizes throughout the paper. Keep it simple, easy to read, and consistent so the reader can follow along. Be sure to double-check formatting and abbreviations for consistency. Also, do not mix and match methods from more than one paper format. For example, if you use MLA parenthetical citations, you cannot use APA citations in your works cited page.

Tip No.

81 If you are struggling with putting together a reference page, ask for samples.

It can take time to get the hang of an unfamiliar style. Online citation makers can help, but they only go so far. If you are confused and overwhelmed, ask your teacher whether they have examples you can look at to help you figure it out.

Sample

Bibliography

1. Archer, Shirley. "For Heart Rate, Tai Chi Comparable to Brisk Walk." *IDEA Fitness Journal* 3, no. 5 (2008): Academic OneFile. [Database online.]

2. Hardy, Annabel, Alice Solomon. "Ki Treatment: Healing with Sound and Touch." *Positive Health Magazine*. 2007, 142.

3. National Center for Complementary and Alternative Medicine. "Tai Chi for Health Purposes." NCCAM Backgrounder. Available from http://nccam.nih.gov/health/taichi. Internet; accessed 25 April 2008.

Tip No.

82 Do not forget to proofread your works cited page or bibliography.

Many students proofread their papers from introduction to conclusion and then neglect their compiled citations. Teachers will read them and dock points for errors here just as much as anywhere else in the paper, so do not forget to give it a once-over.

Study Guide

❏ Formatting is important. Make sure you are aware of any specific formatting requirements, such as margin width, line spacing, and font size, your teacher requires.

❏ If you are having issues figuring out how to adjust the formatting, check the help guide in your processing program.

❏ Be sure you have a word processing program that has all of the features and formatting adjustment tools that you need.

   ❏ If your computer does not come with the Microsoft Office Suite and you cannot afford to purchase it, you can download a free comparable suite from **www.openoffice.org**.

❏ A reference page is a compilation of all of the sources you included in your paper. All your in-text citations should point to full citations in your reference page.

❏ Each style is different, so purchase a style book or bookmark an online style guide for more details on how to compose a reference page in the major styles.

❏ Using an online citation maker can save time. Check out http://citationmachine.net. Be sure to check your citations for accuracy before submitting your paper.

❏ Making your reference page as you write helps you avoid missing citations. If you choose to do it last, make sure you have notes with citation information for all your sources. This is especially important for long papers with many sources.

❏ Do not forget to proofread your reference page. Each style has its own particularities, and you do not want to lose points just because you put a comma in the wrong place.

CHAPTER 12

Proofreading and Editing

Proofreading is the last, but most certainly not least, step in writing a phenomenal paper. As with prewriting and outlining, editing is an all-too-often neglected step of the writing process. Because this is the last step, poor planning often leads to students running out of time to edit. Many high school students have finished a paper the night before it was due, or in a study hall before class, and turned it in still warm from the printer, only to later spot errors they could no longer change. Other students will only run their paper through the digital spell check in their word processor and then call it edited, even when not pressed for time. If this sounds at all like you, now is the time to break yourself of these habits. If this is difficult for you, treat your papers as if they are due a day sooner than they really are, so you can give yourself time to polish it. There are two main categories of editing.

There is editing the content, and there is proofreading, which is editing the mechanics. Both are equally important.

Tip No. 83 **Take a break before beginning the editing and proofreading processes.**

Realistically, this is not always possible. Late night crunches happen to even the most organized students, but try to allow yourself some time to relax before beginning the proofreading process. Walking away from the paper for a little while will give you some distance from what you have written, which will make it easier to spot mistakes. Try getting up for a glass of water, grabbing a snack, taking a short walk, or watching an episode of your favorite TV show before diving into the editing process. This will give your brain some time to cool off so you come back to the paper refreshed and sharp.

Reading for Content

Tip No. 84 **Editing is not just about spelling and grammar.**

Do not forget to read your paper for clarity, focus, word choice, and other content issues before turning it in. Leaving out important details is even worse than mechanical errors, and spell checkers definitely will not catch these types of errors.

This is the first type of editing, Reading for content does not focus on the spelling and grammar, but rather on the actual content and substance of the paper. This type of editing is well beyond the capabilities of spell check. Because editing for content will likely result in your changing, adding, and subtracting parts from your paper, it is best to do this before reading for spelling and grammar. This way you do not miss mechanical errors in any of the rewritten sections of the paper. Editing the content of the paper is not terribly difficult once you know what to look for. With practice, it can be completed quickly and easily.

85 If you were not provided with a rubric, you can make your own.

Many teachers will provide students with a rubric, or a breakdown of what is expected for an assignment, as well as how it will be graded. If your teacher did not provide you with one, you can make your own by summarizing the assignment requirements and then using this checklist as you proofread and edit your paper. You can even ask your teacher what he or she is looking for in the assignment and what aspects might be weighted more heavily and include them in your notes.

Thesis properly supported

How long has it been since you looked at your thesis statement? Depending on the length of the research paper, you have likely spent anywhere from an afternoon to several days writing the body of your paper. Once your writing builds momentum, few people stop and look back at what they have already written. For this reason, some students will barely glance at their thesis until it comes time to restate in the conclusion. This can lead to students leaving out key points mentioned in the thesis or not giving enough support to a point that they might have forgotten was included in their thesis.

Tip No.

86 Highlight sentences that answer your paper's key questions.

Remember way back before you started writing when you were asking yourself the who, what, where, when, why, and how of your topic? A great way to edit your content and ensure you have not left out any key points is to make a list of these questions and then highlight sentences in your paper that address each. You can even highlight different questions in different colors so you can see if there are specific areas that might need more support or that might be focused on more heavily than originally intended.

The easiest and most effective way to ensure you have properly supported your thesis is to get out your thesis and break it down into its main points. Once you have this list, go through your paper one paragraph at a time checking off each of the main points as you find evidence in your paper that supports them.

Once you have completed this, look over the paper and see if there is anything that is either unsupported or under supported. If this is the case, you have two options. You must either rework your thesis statement to make it fit the information the paper actually covers or you must add more supporting information to the body of your paper. Both methods can work equally well. Use your best judgment to decide which is more appropriate.

Tip No. **87** Consider using group study sessions to edit and polish your paper.

Many writing intensive courses require students to break into small groups to brainstorm or peer edit. Too many students blow these off and do not use them as the great resource they are. If you have friends in your class or find a group of like-minded classmates, try setting up times to meet and exchange ideas. It can be helpful to email each other copies of your papers so everyone can look them over and make notes. The peer comments will improve your paper, and helping edit another writer's work will improve your writing as a whole.

If your argument is clear, seems to make a logical progression, and does not feel incomplete, you might be better off reworking your thesis to fit the paper as opposed to trying to add more information. If you are unsure what to do, try enlisting the help of a friend. Ask him or her to make sure the progression of your argument is logical and point out any areas of the paper that seem unclear or confusing. Consider his or her suggestions and make the appropriate changes. Of course, there are other factors to consider as well, such as how long rewriting the paper would take and how much time is left before the deadline. You might also want to consider whether or not changing your paper would require additional research. The length of the paper might also be a factor. Rewriting a two-page paper will take considerably less time than rewriting a ten-page paper. Use your best judgment and evaluate what the best option is based on the time and resources available.

Tip No. 88 Use the "track changes" feature when asking friends to edit your paper or when working on group projects.

Another great feature that too few students are aware of is "track changes." Most word processing programs have this type of feature, so see the program's help menu if you are having trouble locating it. Track changes will highlight and document all changes made to a document, which is great for group projects. It is also a great way to learn from the editing process. Using track changes when you have a friend or tutor proofread your paper will let you know exactly what they changed, and it also gives you the option of either accepting or rejecting the changes they suggest. One thing to keep in mind, however, is that switching between different programs that have this feature (such as different versions of Microsoft Word or Word and OpenOffice) may cause formatting errors. This can happen even when the programs are the same, but it is more common when switching between different programs or operating systems. Also be sure to save your files in a format that can be easily read by multiple programs such as .doc or .rtf.

All research objectives met

The second part of reading for content is to make sure all of your research objectives are met. If each part of your thesis is well supported, you are already halfway to meeting all of your objectives. The other half is making sure all of the requirements listed in the assignment are successfully completed.

Tip No. 89 Use any online resources your school or class might have.

Many schools provide websites for different courses being offered. These websites usually have general information, helpful links, and assignment requirements on them. If your classes have these tools available, bookmark the links so you have this information at your disposal wherever you go.

Go back and reread the assignment sheet. Find any notes you have from when the teacher assigned the paper, if applicable. If you sat down and discussed the assignment with the teacher, make note of everything he or she mentioned. Make a list of all of the requirements for the paper. This includes formatting requirements, source requirements, and page length.

> **Tip No. 90** Before calling your paper finished, be sure to review the requirements of the assignment.
>
> It can be a huge let-down, not to mention extremely stressful, to find out at the end of writing a huge paper that you missed one of the assignment's requirements. Making sure you understand every aspect of an assignment before starting is important, but always be sure to read the assignment over again once you have finished to reassure yourself that everything is covered. It is better to find out now that you need to go back and add details than to find out when you get your grade.

Before submitting your paper, be sure you review this list and double-check that everything on it is completed. This might seem simple, but it will prevent you from making simple, easily fixable mistakes that will cost you points. Failing to do everything required in the assignment, no matter how minor, will change the way the teacher or grader looks at the assignment. Even if it was an honest mistake, whoever is giving you a grade might assume you did not read the assignment carefully enough and might judge everything in your paper more harshly because of it.

91 Save early, and save often.

Tip No.

Do *not* forget to save your paper. If your program has an auto save tool, make sure that it is enabled. Even with that enabled, you should still save your paper whenever you take a break, get up for a glass of water, etc. Make backup copies on a flash drive, external hard drive, in your email inbox, on your cell phone, or some combination of these. There are few things more stressful than losing hours worth of work because of a computer crash, so do not let this happen to you.

CASE STUDY: EDITING TIPS FROM THE WRITING CENTER

Jean Preston
Director, Writing Center, Adjunct
Assistant Teacher of English
Carthage College

I have a bachelor's degree in English and a master's degree in creative writing/poetry, so I have written *many* papers, including two major thesis projects. Since then, for the past six years, I have taught general education college courses, as well as several other writing intensive courses. Therefore, I have extensive experience grading papers.

To properly edit a paper, be sure you understand the assignment and the instructor's expectations. Use any resources available — a writing center, time before or after school when your teachers are available, writing handbook, etc. — to help accomplish writing papers at the proper level.

Talk to a library research specialist about the process he or she is currently using that is unsuccessful (so that ineffective patterns can be identified), and be open to learning new skills to become more successful. Again, take advantage of the resources that are available (and usually free!) at the school.

Remember that 60 percent of errors can be found by reading one's paper out loud. Sentence-level errors are more easily found by reading the essay from end to beginning, sentence by sentence. Proofread several times, concentrating on different issues/errors each time. Keep an "error log" of your most common mistakes, with methods for correction and examples of the right and wrong ways of doing things.

Be sure each paragraph has a solid topic sentence that reflects the thesis and that each paragraph sticks to its topic sentence. Textual support should be gracefully installed and thoughtfully analyzed. Check your conclusion, as well. A good conclusion should restate the thesis, but it should also address the "so what?" question: why was this conclusion/idea/argument important? Also, students often end up introducing an entirely new idea in the conclusion — I try to teach students not to do this.

Also, do not be afraid to go back and significantly change things when you edit. Sometimes, one can write the best introduction *after* the rest of the essay is written. Then, one can design the intro to be both interesting and informative and to really address the content of the paper.

Procrastination is probably the worst enemy of the student writer. Start a project early, and access any helpful resources available to you sooner rather than later.

Grammar, Spelling, and Mechanics

Tip No.

92 Read your paper aloud.

Reading out loud requires a higher level of concentration than reading silently does. You will remain more focused on the words that are actually on the page, which will allow you to spot errors more easily and will also highlight areas that might be clunky or poorly worded. If you stumble reading a section, consider changing it so it rolls off the tongue more cleanly. You can also have a friend or parent read the paper out loud to you. His or her lack of familiarity with the paper will make the rough spots even more obvious.

Once you are satisfied with your paper's content, the next step is checking the spelling, grammar, and other mechanics within the paper. No one wants to get a lower grade because of a misspelled word or forgotten comma. Even students who struggle with spelling and grammar are capable of learning to proof their own writing, so do not fret if mechanics are not your strong suit.

Proofing for errors in basic grammar and mechanics rules

Tip No.

93 Proofread with a screen.
In this case, a screen is a piece of paper or folder you lay over the document you are reading so you can focus on one line at a time. Plain white paper can work just fine for this technique. Use the screen to cover everything below the part you are currently reading, and then move the screen down as you read to reveal more of the document. This forces you to read more slowly and focus on each individual line, which will allow you to catch more errors.

There are several tricks when it comes to proofreading a paper. Many of them seem silly, but techniques such as reading a paper out loud or reading the paper from a print copy, really do make errors easier to spot. Another technique is to read the paper backwards. This can be done by starting from the end of the paper and reading each sentence, one at a time, from the end back to the introduction. This takes the sentences out of context, which will help prevent your brain from going into auto-pilot. You can also read each sentence backwards, starting from either the beginning or end of the paper. For example, "Read each sentence backwards," would be read as "backwards sentence each read." This forces you to look at each word individually, which will make misspellings easier to spot. Try a variety of these techniques to find which ones work best for you.

Tip No. 94 Print your paper out, and read it.

For whatever reason, many people find it easier to spot errors on a hard copy. It might seem like a waste of paper, but if you find yourself constantly missing typos and other errors, try printing your paper out and stepping away from the computer. Mark it up with a red pen, and then take it back to the computer to make the changes, crossing them off on your hard copy as you go.

If you know there are certain words you have trouble spelling or grammatical conventions that give you trouble, try making yourself a cheat sheet to keep by your side as you read your paper. You can then reference this whenever you come across one of your trouble spots or something else that does not look quite right.

Tip No. 95 If you find yourself making the same type of error over and over, make a note of it.

The more you write and edit your papers, the more you will start to notice patterns in your own writing. If you start to see these patterns yourself, or if someone points out a mistake to you that you have made several times, write it down so you can remember it and avoid making it in the future.

The following tables can also be used as reference. They contain some of the most common errors people make when writing.

Common Mistakes	Correct Usage Explanation
Your and You're confusion	"Your" is a possessive word indicating ownership. (ex. Do not forget your bag.)
	"You're" is a contraction of the words "you" and "are." (ex. Are you sure you're going to come with us to the movie?)
Its and It's confusion	"Its" with no apostrophe is the possessive form of the pronoun "it." (ex. The dog wagged its tail.)
	"It's" is a contraction of the words "it" and "is." (ex. It's really hot out today.)
There, Their, and They're confusion	"There" is used to indicate a place. (ex. Do not park there.)
	"Their" is the possessive of the pronoun "they." (ex. We got here in their car.)
	"They're" is a contraction of the words "they" and "are." (ex. They're bringing the car.)
Comma splices	Comma splices occur when two complete thoughts are improperly joined with a comma, which creates a run-on sentence.
	"We decided to go to the movies, we saw the new comedy film." is a comma splice and can be corrected by placing either a period or a semicolon in place of the comma or putting a conjunction such as "and" after the comma.

Pronoun disagreement	Pronoun disagreement occurs when a pronoun does not correctly match the noun it replaces. This most commonly occurs when a plural noun is being used. "Your teacher will tell you what they want in the assignment" is an example of this. The pronoun (they) is plural, but the noun it is referring to (teacher) is singular. This can be corrected by either changing "teacher" to "teachers" or by changing "they" to "he or she" if the gender is unknown or choosing one if the gender is known.
Tense disagreement	Tense disagreement occurs when a shift is made between past, present, or future tense for no reason. In the sentence "When she drove to work, she goes past the gas station." is incorrect. The section before the comma is in past tense, but the part after the comma is in present tense. To fix this, either change "drove" to "drives" or change "goes" to "went."
Improper semicolon use	The semicolon (;) is one of the most misused punctuation marks. Semicolons are used to join two complete thoughts that are closely related. They are not a replacement for commas or for a period if the two thoughts are unrelated. A semicolon can take the place of a comma and conjunction when it is joining two complete thoughts. It can also take the place of a period that separates two complete, but related, sentences. (ex. We went to the movies last night; we saw the new comedy film.)

This is not a complete list by any means, but it is a starting point. If there are other mechanics rules that give you trouble, feel free to add to this table.

Tip No. **96** Try reading your paper in reverse (Or: reverse in paper your reading try).

By this point, you have likely read and reread your paper dozens of times, which makes proofreading problematic. You have read the material so much that you miss errors because you subconsciously change what a sentence actually says to what it should say. Starting at the back end and working your way to the front is a great way to avoid this. To proofread for spelling, look at your paper backward, one word at a time. For grammar, do the same thing, but read by sentence.

Using automated grammar and spell checkers

Tip No. **97** Do not rely on spell checkers to edit your paper.

In a digital age where so many basic tasks are automated, it can be easy to rely on your computer's spell and grammar check functions to do your editing for you. Although these tools do make it easy to spot misspellings and other errors, they are far from foolproof. Do use these tools, but still look the paper over with your own eyes to catch misplaced words or spelling errors the computer misses.

Automated spell and grammar checks are both a blessing and a curse to students. These tools are standard in word processing programs and will catch the majority of spelling errors and even some grammatical errors, depending on the sophistication of the software.

Although these are usually a great help because they make errors easy to spot, they will miss things. For example, if you mistype a word, but the error happens to be the correct spelling of another word, spell check will not flag this. For example, if you tried to type "gear" but accidentally hit the "F" key, which is next to the "G" key on a standard QWERTY keyboard, you will spell "fear." Depending on the context, spelling and grammar checks will likely miss this completely. Mistakes like this happen frequently, so be sure to keep your eyes open for them. Even when a word is flagged as a misspelling, it can be easy to click on the wrong suggested word, as most of the time the program will make several guesses as to what you meant to type. Some of these programs will even attempt to automatically correct errors or predict words as you type, which is useful until it automatically corrects a misspelling to the wrong word without you noticing. In short, these tools are a great time saver, but they are not a replacement for reading over a paper with your own eyes.

Tip No.

98 Add technical words to your word processor's dictionary.
Depending on your subject, you might find terms that your computer does not recognize. Spell checkers might catch chemical compounds, proper nouns, and other jargon, even when they are spelled right. Be sure you do have the spelling right, and then add these words to your word processor's dictionary. This will make it easier to avoid misspelling these words throughout the paper.

Other Resources for Polishing a Paper

Tip No. **99** Make yourself aware of dictionary functions and other helpful tools on your computer.

Computers are wonderful tools, even when not being used to their fullest potential. Most computers and computer programs come preloaded with features that make writing and editing much easier. One of these functions is the dictionary tool, which will allow you to look up the definition of an unknown word. The dictionary function might also include thesaurus information, which is useful when trying to edit out trite phrases and overused words.

If your school offers on-site writing help or access to tutors, book an appointment to get help with editing your paper. These resources are almost always free and will vastly improve your writing in a short amount of time. If you have a paper due during a busy time, such as midterms or finals, be sure to book an appointment well in advance, as they fill up quickly.

Tip No. **100** Use the "find" function in your word processor to help you edit quickly.

Most word processors have an awesome feature called "find" or "find and replace." This tool can make some types of editing much quicker and easier. For example, using the find feature to locate all apostrophes in a document will highlight any contractions that you might have accidentally used. If you tend to overuse particular words, you can use "find" to locate them and make the appropriate changes. Consider making a list of words you know you want to avoid using, or over-using, and then search your document for each of them. This is a great, quick way to improve your paper.

You also might consider looking into software that can analyze your word use frequency. These programs will take a text, analyze it, and then make a list of the most commonly used words in it. This, combined with a thesaurus, will improve your writing and your vocabulary. Programs such as this can be purchased or downloaded from the Internet either for free or for a small price. A good example of a web-based application can be found at **http://rainbow.arch.scriptmania.com/tools/word_counter. html**. Hermetic Systems also has a program that you can download from their website (**www.hermetic.ch/wfc/wfc.htm**) that will analyze word frequency. There is a trial of the program available, or you can pay for the full version. These are only two examples, but a quick search of the Internet should point you in the direction of several more programs and websites, as well as plug-ins you can install with your office suite to make them capable of analyzing word frequency. Just be aware that with many of the online applications, there is a maximum word count that can be analyzed, or analyzing a huge document may cause the website to time out. Because of this, these applications are generally better suited to smaller research papers than full-blown dissertations.

Tip No. **101** Relax, and congratulate yourself on a job well done.

You have reached the finish line! Your paper is done, still warm from the printer and ready to turn in or possibly already in the hands of your teacher. Do not stress out about the grade you will receive; try to move on and focus ahead on the  next assignment. Even if you do not do as well as you had hoped on this assignment, treat it as a learning experience. Ask yourself what you can do differently next time, and take constructive criticism to heart.

Study Guide

❑ There are two main types of proofreading/editing. These are editing for content and editing for mechanics/spelling/grammar.

❑ When proofreading for content, try to highlight sentences that answer your paper's key questions.

❑ Consider using group study sessions to edit and polish your paper. Your friends will catch errors you might miss.

❑ Use the "track changes" feature when asking friends to edit your paper or when working on group projects.

❑ Do not call the paper finished until you review the requirements of the assignment and make sure it meets all of them.

❑ When proofreading for mechanical errors, try the following:

   ❑ Print your paper out and read it.
   ❑ Read your paper aloud.
   ❑ Try reading your paper in reverse.
   ❑ Do not rely on spell check to edit your paper.
   ❑ Proofread with a screen.
   ❑ Use the "find" function in your word processor to help you edit quickly. This is useful for finding overused words so they can be replaced.

❑ Always take a break before beginning the editing and proofreading process.

❑ Remember that formatting is part of the editing process, so make sure you check your formatting and how the paper looks on the page, too.

❏ Holding the paper upside-down can help with this, as you will catch layout errors you otherwise might miss.

CONCLUSION:

The Road to Success is a Rocky One

As with most things in life, there is a large measure of trial and error involved in learning to write well. Some students will find that the writing process comes easily once they learn the basics. Others will struggle with developing a style and learning how to construct a strong, logical argument. Even students who have natural writing talent make mistakes and experience pitfalls that come from a lack of experience. Knowing what teachers are looking for, and, more importantly, how to find out what teachers want to see is just as important as your skill level.

Students who have a history of producing well-written and highly praised papers in middle school, or early high school classes, will still struggle in advanced classes if they do not understand what their instructors are looking for. Standards are higher in high school (and even higher in college), and impressing teachers is just as much about being able to say something novel and different as it is about being able to say something well. There will be ups and downs, as each instructor is likely to have personal standards and expectations that you will have to adapt to. An "A" worthy paper for one teacher might only be "B" quality to another.

The important thing to remember is that writing great papers is a *skill*. It is something that you can learn how to do, though it might take a lot of time and hard work. The best, and really only, way to improve your writing is by practicing. With each assignment you complete, you will get better. If you do not do as well on one assignment as you had hoped, learn what you can from the experience so you will have more skills at your disposal next time. Over time, you will find that adapting your writing to fit different academic situations will get easier.

In the end, you will be glad you acquired these skills, regardless of your major or field of study. With the globalization of society and prevalence of the Internet, email, and other digital communications, being able to write well is more important than ever. The skills you develop now by researching, compiling, and condensing information, formulating a well-thought out argument, and expressing your thoughts and ideas clearly on paper are valuable skills that will serve you well, no matter where life takes you.

CASE STUDY: FINAL ADVICE

Name: Mary Smith
Job Title: Former Substitute Teacher
I substitute taught at the
junior high and high school
level and worked with my own
children helping them with their
papers through high school.

For many students, now is the first time they are asked to come up with their own topics of interest and write more lengthy papers. Pick a topic that is interesting to you. You will be more likely to have original ideas and research more thoroughly. Do preliminary research to ensure your topic has enough supporting material for your ideas.

Use the preliminary research to pick out and begin collecting further research on five to ten key ideas. It is important not to exclude any at this point to allow ideas and the direction of the paper to fully develop.

A thesis statement should be a broad enough statement that catches the readers' attention and peaks their interest in the topic to be covered in the paper.

As a historian, I always tried to use a primary source. If you use secondary sources, you are relying on their research methods, which may have been incorrect. Also, primary sources lead to more interesting ideas and originality. Look at Xlibris (**www.xlibris.com**), a popular online self-publishing site. You can find authors and information that have more limited distribution, thus opening up less used sources.

I am of the old school of notecards. I still feel that it is a very valid way of both developing information and tracking sources. I feel it allows the writer to take good ideas and information and store it for future use as the paper is developing. It keeps the writer from forgetting where an idea may have been or come from. It also allows the writer to reorganize ideas as the paper develops. Often a source point may be more applicable to somewhere not originally intended and with a notecard, it is easy to move around while maintaining information citing requirements.

Begin researching early. The research will always take longer than you think. Also, allow sufficient time for rewriting. Getting initial drafts down on paper early allows you to leave the paper for a while and come back with fresh new ideas.

When editing, read the paper out loud. We are so much more tuned in to how things sound that mistakes can be glaring when heard even to your own ear. Beware of relying totally on spell-checkers. If you spell something right, but it is not the word you intended, it won't be picked up.

APPENDIX A:

Sample Research Papers

The following are two sample research papers. The first was written as an argumentative assignment for an advanced composition class. The second was written for a unit on world religions as an informative paper. The first one is annotated for you, with commentary similar to what someone grading the paper might write, in order to highlight specific things the student did well, and what the student could improve on, and explain the way the paper is structured.

The second one has room for you to try your hand at annotating the paper by either making a copy of the pages or writing right in the book. Try your hand at it and see if you can recognize the parts of a research paper and what about the paper is done well. Being able to recognize these things will go a long way towards improving your own writing.

Both of these papers are presented in MLA format, though the citations could easily be changed to comply with other styles.

Erika Eby
Name Of Teacher
Class Title
Date

Animania and Manga Madness   ◀ Catchy title!

    Saturday morning channel surfing normally entails   ◀ Good opening
bits and pieces of news flashing past, as well as flashes   sentence
of color and animated figures being silly to entertain   and a strong
millions of kids. Nickelodeon, Cartoon Network,   introduction.
and The Disney Channel all show cartoons for hours
on end. Some even play them twenty-four hours a
day. However, recently a new type of animation has
been filtering into televisions all over the world. With
brightly colored characters, insanely huge eyes, and
many other oddities, they are very different from most
American made cartoons. "Pokemon," "Speed Racer,"
and "Sailor Moon" are good examples of Japanese
anime, which has been slowly making its way into the
big time. Anime, Japanese animations, and manga,
Japanese comic books, are becoming increasingly
popular among American children, teens, and even
adults. The Reason? Japanese anime and manga are
better than American cartoons.

    The history of anime and manga is an interesting
one, and one of the many things that makes the
Japanese cartooning industry so grand. Granted, the
Japanese did not start seriously cartooning until after
the Americans, but they took the art and changed it

into something of their own in the early twentieth century when two big Western innovations came into being: the newspaper comic strip and the motion picture. Soon after, Japanese artists were making comics that would pave the way for the manga of the future. The comic artists in Japan began to experiment with animated motion pictures, but did not achieve world-wide success at it until Kitayama Seitaro's short film *Momotaro* in 1918. Slowly, the foundation for anime was being laid, but true anime would not show up until after WWII (O'Connell).

◀ **"Pave the way" is okay, but maybe a more graphically inclined metaphor?**

◀ **Good transition!**

After the war, unbelievably, the start and success of both anime and manga rested on the shoulders of one man: Osamu Tezuka. Originally, Tezuka was an animator, but he started cartooning after WWII, and at the age of twenty he produced hist first significant work, a novel length comic called *Shintakarajima* or "New Treasure Island." Tezuka basically invented the anime or manga style of art and story-telling techniques. He packed his stories with action and emotion and stretched his stories out for hundreds of pages using techniques from the French and German cinemas. Scenes would unfold slowly, spanning several pages, much like they would in a film. All this and more made Tezuka the most popular manga artist in Japan and earned him the undisputed title "The God of Manga" (O'Connell).

◀ **What techniques? Some specifics would be nice here.**

His art reflected his story telling and is his most obvious contribution to the anime and manga scene. He designed his characters to make it easier to portray wide ranges of emotion. Although his style at first may seem simple and cartoonish, the big round heads and huge expressive eyes actually allows character drawn this way to express every emotion, from pure joy to passionate hatred. It does make sense to emphasize the face of the characters when all an artist has to express emotion is that image. Every emotion conceivable can be expressed just by moving the parts of the face. Because the style was so good at expressing emotions, other artist used the same principles in their art. All modern anime characters have this man to thank for their sleek and stylish looks (O'Connell).

Tezuka was not alone in his cartooning. Several others made their own adaptations to his storytelling and art styles and took off with stories of their own, and with the help of Hiroshi Okawa the stories in manga made it onto the big screen. His studio, Toei Animation, started producing movies similar to those coming out of Disney Studios in America. The first feature length animation to come out of Toei was *The Tale of the White Serpent* and was considerably darker than your typical Disney film, but it paved the way for the more serious and mature anime and manga of the future (O'Connell).

Tezuka eventually entered the anime scene working with Toei. First he animated stories based on legend and other people's works. He later founded his own animation company and began work on some soon to be internationally famous works based on his own mangas. *Tetsuwan Atom*, or Astro Boy, missed out on being the first domestically produced animated TV show in Japan by just a few months, but it was the first regularly animated TV show with a reoccurring cast. *Jungle Taitei*, or Kimba the White Lion, had an American co-producer and NBC helped to finance the project. Unfortunately, that limited the creative scope of the show, making it more like an American cartoon than anything else, but it became very popular just the same. The anime did stir up some controversy after *The Lion King* was released because of several striking similarities that may suggest that Disney copied the idea from Tezuka (Zagzoug).

◀ **An explaination of "more like an American cartoon" would be helpful.**

Disney and Tezuka did have a few similarities. It is safe to say that Tezuka was like the Japanese version of Disney and vice versa. Both of them paved the way for future aspiring animators and cartoonists, and both of them also invented their own style and were among the first to explore feature length animation. Many American cartoonists were propaganda artists during the war, as were many Japanese artists. Propaganda was pretty much the first use for cartoonists, and it is probably what sparked the interest in animation worldwide (Zagzoug). Disney and other Americans may have started it, but they inspired people like Tezuka who took that idea and make it into something new and exciting.

The most well-known and noticeable difference between anime and manga and American cartoons is the style of art used. Of course, no two artists draw anime exactly the same, and they all have developed their own styles, some more realistic and some more fantasy-like, but generally all anime and manga art is highly influenced by the art of Tezuka. True, a lot of anime style characters have gravity defying hair styles in neon colors, and impossibly large and wildly colored eyes, making some of them appear very fantasy-like, but at least all of them have five fingers (Hadad).

Anime characters tend to follow specific formulas. A typical anime female has big round eyes that normally have lots of shine or white spots. Their hair is normally big and looks as if they emptied about five cans of hairspray into it, but it may also be pulled back, braided, or very short. They normally have a gorgeous figure with plenty of curves, a tiny waist, long legs, and maybe a large chest to boot. This formula will change depending on the artist and the character's role in the story. For example, if the character were evil their eyes might be smaller and less shiny compared to a young and innocent school girl (Zagzoug).

◄ Should be "her eyes," watch your pronoun agreement!

A different formula applies to males. Many of them either have enormously huge muscles or are skinny like sticklike figures. Their eyes are are still huge compared to a normal human, but small compared to most females, although if the male in question is a child then their eyes are normally bigger. A lot of males also have longer hair than their female co-stars, or at least have more than the stereotypical male. Again, this formula changes based on the artist and the type of character they are. There are a lot of character and artists that do not follow these formulas, but most of the more famous characters are drawn this way (Zagzoug).

◀ "his eyes." Watch the pronoun agreement!

◀ Good specifics.

Often in manga, and sometimes in anime, an artist will use a "Chibi" or Super Deformed version of a character in order to portray a certain feeling or scene. A Chibi is very small and childlike with an every with an even bigger head and even larger eyes than a regular anime person. A time when an artist may use a Chibi would be when the character is crying or extremely happy. Sometimes the Chibi is just used to make a character appear cuter or more naïve than usual. Also, in manga, a Chibi takes up less space than a typically drawn character, which comes in handy when the artist only has so much space on the page (Hadad).

◀ Some details about any parallels in American cartoons might be helpful here.

One of the things about Japanese anime and manga that makes the artistry better than most American cartoons is the detail and time put into drawing every scene. The hair is often drawn to show strands and chunks of the hair and extra attention is spent in drawing clothing folds to make everything seem accurate. The detail in their animation is unparalleled. "Cell Style Animation" is used to put almost every part of a scene on a different layer so when moving something it may be only one layer that is changed. For example, if the character looks in a different direction all that needs to be done is to change the eye later around. In their "Mecha" anime, or anime that have to do with robots, every piston and digital display is drawn and animated. Anime always animates the shadows and highlights, unlike many American cartoons, some of which are not even shaded. The subtle detail and animation puts anime a huge step above American animation, which is much more straight forward. If something is supposed to move, it moves, and less attention is spent on animated the faces of characters (Hadad).

With anime, a huge amount of effort is spent on animating the face. When characters a purposely designed so they can show such a wide range of emotions, it would be silly not to. Often in anime everything will be still except a character's face or everything will be still in the foreground while the background moves. This is easily achieved with Cell Style Animation. Anime and manga do use bold movements and dramatic poses like American cartoons, but the poses are not copied from Americans. They are actually similar to posing used in Kabuki Theater (Hadad).

◄ **Another good transition.**

The American cartoonists do pay the same attention to detail on some of the higher end productions, but the style of art and animation is much less uniform. Some may attempt to make everything as realistic as possible with well-formed characters and huge amounts of detail put into backgrounds, like in the works of Disney and in Marvel comics. Others may barely resemble the human figure with odd shaped heads, off-colored skin, and large noses. As far as animation, the westerners take a more direct approach and animate almost everything. Americans pride themselves on making their animations as fluid as possible, but, when you have every element on the screen moving, it can become a distraction because there is also usually background music and a plot to follow (Hadad).

It is important to note that the anime style and the idea for making cartoons was not taken entirely from the West. The Japanese have been making stylized, or cartoonish, art for hundreds of years, and some of the older drawings bear some resemblance to modern Japanese anime style art. True, Osamu Tezuka and other important Japanese manga artists were inspired by Disney and Fleisher, but the main elements that comprise the anime style, such as simple lines and stylized features, are very Japanese (Izawa).

◀ I had a teacher that banned the phrase "It is important to note." Was he right? A stronger phrasing might be useful.

The art is not the only thing that puts anime and manga above American cartoons. The content of anime and manga has a much broader range. Just about any theme can be found, from adult content to educational children's material. This may seem more than surprising when compared to the anime shown on television in America. It is important to remember that when an anime is translated into English, a lot of the original content is changed and some lines are edited. Most televised anime was originally rated PG-13, but it was edited in the translation and make more kid-friendly (Zagzoug). However, a lot of people want a taste of anime how it was meant to be shown, so they buy copies of the shows with English subtitles or dubbed copies that have not been edited (Kim).

◀ **You are using too many general words. Avoid "a lot."**

Even the anime and manga intended for children tend to be more complex and mature than most American cartoons. They often depict death and serious issues for the protagonists to deal with, whereas most American cartoons made for children skirt around some of these realities of life. The characters are very complex as well and have serious flaws. They may be loud and annoying, or be unpopular and depressed. Some of them are extremely ditzy and others take everything way too seriously. The villains are not always pure evil or insane and often have goals other than destroying the world, or they help friends and loved ones. In the show "Yu-Gi-Oh!" the main villain, Pegasus, is trying to collect items that would allow him to control the world, in the process stealing the souls of several innocent people, but he does this because he lost the love of his life shortly after they were married and thinks that if he can get these items he can bring her back. Technology is also portrayed sympathetically or at least in a more complex fashion than in America (Izawa).

The Japanese are not afraid to explore topics that are normally ignored in other animation, such as technology. The stories address sensitive issues for most people, like religion, death, addiction, and child abuse. In the manga and anime "Chobits" by CLAMP, a female ground of manga artists, the plot addresses humanoid robots that act like and even replace humans. It brings up the issues of humans falling in love with robots, robots falling in love with humans, and robots falling in love with each other. The Japanese do not pull punches when it comes to these subjects. Another popular anime, "Serial Experiments Lain," deals with suicide, addiction, and the draw and power the Internet has on people, and that's just in the first four episodes. The characters encounter sensitive and emotional problems and have to deal with them, which makes for very powerful storytelling (Jett).

While some American cartoons are aimed at adults, most are purely for children. The characters are simple and the plots even more so. The main characters are almost always good and pire of heart. Typically they never make the wrong decision at a critical moment and end up losing something or someone close to them or even get themselves killed. Their victories are always complete and with little or no repercussions. The villains are often doing evil actions for no reason other than they are bad people, and they are usually defeated in the end. In most cases they are also packed with simple humor is very easy to grasp. True, they are aimed at children, but a little mental stimulation would not hurt them. Shows like *The Simpsons* and *South Park* are slowly starting to change that. While they still often have childish humor in them, they are normally packed with just as much social satire, if not more (Hadad).

The biggest content difference between the Japanese and American cartoons is probably the one that sets anime and manga the farthest above American cartooning. In America most cartoon characters are forced into one short-lived plot after another, whereas in anime and manga the plots often come from the everyday lives of the characters and are character driven. They character may have to fight an evil force or save the world, but often times they also have friends and family problems, homework, school, hobbies, and personal goals to deal with. While episodes or chapters might be dedicated to a character's personal issues or a part of their daily schedule, like work or school, and the small-scale problems faced there. Everything that happens has a foundation in reality that makes the stories exciting, relatable, and real (Izawa).

Another presence in anime and manga that adds realism is the changes that take place. Bad people can improve or change their ways. They may find redemption. Good people might go through something that makes them stray from the good path. Characters learn and gain wisdom and insights that change them forever. Even if the character does not win, and they do not win all the time, they still earn something valuable. In fact, in many anime or manga the hero dies after winning, or gets what they want but loses something important to them in the process. Either way, the plot is deep and satisfying (Izawa).

Japanese anime and manga are sweeping the globe and are giving American cartoons a run for their money. It all started with Osamu Tezuka and his visions that changed the cartooning industry forever. His works are regarded on the same level as those of Disney and Fleisher, but with a Japanese twist to them. His drawing inspired a while new style of art that is still alive and prospering today. Huge heads and eyes couple with simple likes and stylized features make the anime and manga style a sight to behold. His emotional and dramatic way of storytelling also rubbed off on others, making the stories in anime and manga what they are today. These character driven plots with real conflicts and relatable character make the anime scene truly enticing to people around the world. People are portrayed as people with faults, dreams, and goals, not stereotype driven do-gooders running around saving the day. The villains are people too, a lot of time just normal people ◀ **Avoid "a lot!"** who are not that different from the protagonists. The heroes sometimes die or do not get what they want. These ideas and techniques are slowly starting to show up in cartoons in other countries around the world, and it is high time cartoons got a little more cultured. Anime and manga may be labeled as a fad and die out over the course of the next few years, but the impact that they have had on the cartooning industry will show for years to come.

◀ **Well-put. Good final sentence.**

Works Cited

Hadad, Ivan and Hiten Patel. <u>Anime and American Cartoons</u> 24 Nov, 2003 <http://www.honors.uiuc.edu.ealc15097/Hiten-Ivan/cartoons.htm>.

Izawa, Eri. <u>What are Manga and Anime?</u> 1995. 16 Dec. 2003 <http://www.mit.edu:8001/people/rei/Expl.html>.

Jett, Jennifer. "The Art of Powerful Storytelling." <u>Arizona Daily Star.</u> From <u>Electric Library.</u>

Kim, Michael. <u>Japanese Animation</u> 25 Jan. 1996. 17 Dec. 2003. <http://alumni.imsa.edu/~leda/anime/>.

O'Connell, Michael. <u>A Brief History of Anime</u> 19 Nov. 2003 <http://www.corneredangle.com/anwess.history.htm>.

Zagzoug, Marwah. <u>The History of Anime and Manga</u> Apr. 2000. 21 Nov. 2003 <http://novaonline.nvcc.vccs.edu/eli/evans/his/35/events/anime02/anime62.html> .

Cons: Watch your pronoun-anteceedent agreement! Avoid using too many general terms like "a lot."

Pros: A great paper. Save it for future reference. It is very clear and direct.

Erika Eby
Name of Course
Name of Teacher
Date

Paganism in the Age of Information

Most people have been exposed, at some point in their lives, to relics of ancient religions, be it via tales of the escapades of the Greek and Roman pantheons or through learning about Egyptian mummification practices. There is something oddly captivating and awe inspiring about monuments such as the Parthenon at Athens and Stonehenge in Britain. Images of these relics along with Druid priests in long flowing robes and rural Shamans taking spiritual journeys are what often come to mind when people talk of Paganism. New Age revivals of many ancient Pagan spiritual beliefs, however, have put a modern twist on ancient Druidism and Shamanism. Entirely new religions have even risen from the revival of these ancient spiritual practices, such as Wicca. The modern urban and suburban culture may seem to undermine the simplistic lifestyle many think of in association with paganism, not to mention hinder the focus of these religions on the beauty and power found within nature. If nature is such a key part of Pagan beliefs, how is it that Paganism is not only surviving, but in some cases thriving, in the modern urban environments? Though the urban and suburban world, with its hectic nature and technological advancements, requires some adaptation to Pagan practices, the religions still honor and celebrate their ancient counterparts with a modern twist.

One of the most sacred parts of most Pagan religions is ritual and spell work. Spell craft in the modern Pagan perspective is different from the magic one might read about in fantasy novels. Rituals to honor the divine and the cycles of nature are comparable to a Christian attending church on Sunday. Going with that same metaphor, magic (or "magick," as some call it to distinguish it from stage magic) is similar to a Christian prayer. It is believed that if one focuses his or her desires, he or she can alter the flow of energy and make those desires manifest. The changes, however, are small things. "You're never going to shoot lightning from your fingertips, nor will you win the lottery because you lit a green candle. And you're certainly not going to become the Big Pooh-Bah of Magic because you picked up a copy of spells from some Big Name Pagan," (Beyer). Spell casting is often combined with ritual and is used for protection, healing, and divine guidance, not for putting "hexes" on one's enemies.

Many aspects of modern Pagan religions overlap with Christian traditions and holidays. This helps add to the allure of these New Age religions and is one of the many reasons modern urban people are starting to convert to Paganism. Many Pagans have the misconception that the reason for these similarities is because Christians desecrated and stole traditions from other Pre-Christian religions. This, however, is simply because of the way religions evolve and spread over time. "...Certainly the overlap of holidays and locations helped ease the transition, but it was not an overnight process, nor were the formerly pagan communities without a hand in all this. Religion is an evolving thing. Even when new ideas are accepted, old ones are not easily set aside like last week's newspaper, and the Church was wise in recognizing this fact," (Beyer). By the same principle, the reverse is proving true in modern culture. The similarities between Christianity and Paganism play a part in the effectiveness of modern Pagan movements, as well as Paganism's adaptability to the modern world.

Part of the adaptability that makes Paganism appealing in modern city-dwelling culture is the lack of universalized formalities and formal scriptures. There is no book that tells Pagans how to celebrate their holidays or how to worship their deities, so practices can vary greatly from practitioner to practitioner. There are some Pagans who feel there is a proper order and set of materials required to effectively hold rituals and perform spells, but there is also a growing number of Pagans who disagree and show ways to make magic simple and affordable. Kaldera and Schwartzstein are among them: "You have to have everything from the proper set of thousand-dollar robes to the right stuff in your stomach to a pharmacopoeia of obnoxious, illegal herbs and (ugh!) dried animal bits from obscure third-world countries...Sorry, wrong again. (Unless that kind of thing really turns you on.)," (Kaldera 9). If complex ritual is something that appeals to a particular Pagan, that is fine, but there are ways to draw on the energy and power of everyday items and junk found in the city as well.

Because of the idea that a Pagan does not necessarily need to spend a fortune on spell working tools, Paganism is evolving into a more and more "practical" religion, so to speak. City-dwellers who do not have time to regularly attend church or adhere to a strict religious timetable may find Paganism appealing. "Urban Primitives" is a term that is starting to be applied to Pagans who use the city for their religious workings. They adhere to the idea that much of ancient religious practices were about survival in a harsh environment, so adapted practices today should apply to survival in the urban environment. They may be strapped for cash and go dumpster diving for ceremonial tools or use common city weeks for spell work. With many of the principles of magic relying on the concept of directing energy and cities being places with lots of energy, it seems logical for there to be some Pagans who choose to harness this energy as well as the energy of the natural world (Kaldera 1-7).

By this same token, a growing number of practitioners of magic are abandoning their personal altars and elaborate ritual preparations and taking magic to the streets. Many believe that in today's world, asking for the help of the deities or focusing energy to create change should be able to be done "on the go" as needed. In other words, it should be able to be used practically. "If magic works, then it should work as well on the street as it does in the temple...Performing practical magic is an exercise in self-trust," (Dunn 139). There seems to be a call for, in today's society, a way to connect with the divine anywhere and to effectively take some sort of action and gain some control over an individual's own fate during the crazy ebb and flow of day to day life in the 21st century.

Many modern Pagans are also embracing technology in a way that other religions are not. Computers and the Internet are considered by some to be viable ritual tools or ways of communing with the divine. Technology is becoming an integral part of daily life, from computers to cars, and that is not looking to change. Anything that a person uses regularly starts to take on that person's personal energy, making it a powerful item. Many pagans also commune or "invoke" spirits or deities in their rituals, for example, calling upon a particular goddess or the elements for help. The elements can be contacted through modern incarnations of them according to urban Pagans. For example, phone lines and modems house air spirits, power lines are linked to fire, and plumbing or drinking fountains are linked with water (Kaldera 71-79). Going along with this line of thought, modems and the Internet are sacred to some.

Some Pagans take this a step further and actually hold religious ceremonies in chat rooms, in some cases. Not all Pagans do this, but some who live in isolated areas or who do not know others who they feel comfortable worshiping with in their area, find it easier to fit online ritual into their schedule (Kaldera 179-181). This has caused some tension in the Pagan community, as some feel that something as "unnatural" as the

Internet should not be viewed as a divine medium. Others feel that their ancestors were focused on survival and would embrace the new technology. Regardless, the Internet is a widespread means for communication and for the sharing of information, which is integral to Pagan religions. "As the information superhighway embraces ever-increasing levels of intensity, I believe many magical devotees will feel powerfully drawn towards embracing the new technology in all its diversity. Sacred shrines and archetypal symbols will find a richer and mover convincing graphic expression on the Internet so that they really do become magical doorways in their own right..." (Drury 100). Despite the arguments for and against such use, the embracing of the Internet in some Pagan communities is an adaptation of these religions to better equip them for survival in the 21st century.

Even without the use of technology, many Pagans are starting to evolve the faces of their gods and goddesses to ones that are more helpful in day to day city life. Simple spells are performed to avoid traffic, and some may call on a deity to find a parking spot. These things may seem trivial, but to those who are trying to hold down a job, they can be important to survival. The idea of "triple deities" is important to Wicca and many other Pagan traditions. Deities of old such as Zeus, Artemis, and Loki are called upon by many to aid in goals or ritual work. On other occasions, one of the faces of a triple deity may be called on (i.e. The traditional triple goddess has three faces: Maid, Mother, and Crone). An example of an urban revamp of these deities would be the goddesses "Squat," "Skor," and "Skram" or the gods "Slick," "Screw," and "Sarge." Squat may be called upon to ensure a parking spot, Skram tells you when you need to leave a dangerous area, and Sarge is a god to help give you motivation to get a job done. This may seem silly and almost sacrilegious to some, but in Paganism, the focus is more on the energy that is in everything on Earth than the names associated with it. The tools and names used to call upon the divine, which is viewed as a manifestation of that energy, are just things to help the practitioners focus their wills and intents (Kaldera 55-68).

Many modern Pagan practices are quite different from what is believed to be the traditions of ancient Pre-Christian religions, but there are still similarities. Many of the differences that some Pagans embrace have come about as adaptations of these old practices in order to make them more applicable to the modern world. This easy adaptability due to the individualism emphasized within the various Pagan traditions is one of the many reasons Paganism is still surviving in modern cities and urban environments. Many of the practices are also similar enough to major religions, and most people have heard enough about the lore of ancient pantheons of gods to make converting to Paganism easy for those with the desire. Ancient Pagan practices may not be completely compatible with the modern world, but the Neopagan movement is evolving into a religion with the capacity to thrive in this fast paced urban world.

<u>Works Cited:</u>

Beyer, Catherine Noble. <u>Wicca For the Rest of Us.</u> 2002. Timerift Network. <www.wicca.timerift.net>

Drury, Nevill. "Magic and Cyberspace." <u>Esoterica</u> 2002: 96-100.

Dunn, Patrick. <u>Postmodern Magic: The Art of Magic in the Information Age.</u> St. Paul: Llewellyn Publications, 2005.

Kaldera, Raven and Tannin Schwartzstein. <u>The Urban Primitive: Paganism in the Concrete Jungle.</u> St. Paul: Llewellyn Publications, 2002.

APPENDIX B:
Helpful Links

Son of Citation machine
http://citationmachine.net

Purdue OWL (Online Writing Lab)
http://owl.english.purdue.edu

Modern Language Association
www.mla.org

Chicago Manual of Style
www.chicagomanualofstyle.org

OpenOffice
www.openoffice.org

LibreOffice
www.libreoffice.org

Google Scholar
http://scholar.google.com

Google Documents
http://docs.google.com

Microsoft Academic Search

http://academic.research.microsoft.com

Citation Manager with add-on for Firefox

www.zotero.org

Refseek

www.refseek.com

APPENDIX C:
Glossary

Abstract – An abstract, sometimes called a Précis or Synopsis, is a brief summary of an article, analysis, or other in-depth dissertation on a particular subject. Abstracts are often found at the beginning of scholarly articles to give readers a succinct overview of what the article will cover. Some large research projects might require students to write an abstract. An abstract generally includes an explanation of the topic, the research methods used, the results, and a hint as to the conclusions drawn from the research.

Acknowledgment – A section, usually in the beginning, of many books or other longer works in which the author credits others who have helped shape his or her work. This can sometimes be useful in research because it explains where the author drew help or inspiration and might lead to ideas for other sources to research.

Annotated bibliography – A bibliography that includes an evaluation or summary of each source listed. These are often used to ensure a student has properly researched a topic and validated all sources used.

Article - a written piece that explores a specific topic. Articles are generally an independently written part of a periodical, such as a newspaper, journal, or magazine.

Autobiography - A biographical work that was written by the person who is the subject of the biography. These are primary sources and often offer insights that biographies do not, but some authors might exaggerate or bend the truth to make a better story, so their credibility should still be examined.

Bibliography - Sometimes called a Works Cited page, a bibliography is a list of all sources used in a research paper, article,

or other document. The format of this will vary depending on the type of style being used.

Biography - A work written to contain factual historical information about the life and times of a particular person, or occasionally persons. Biographies are secondary sources because they are not written by the subject of the biography but are rather researched by an author and compiled.

Blog - An abbreviation for "Web Log," blogs are increasing in popularity and are widespread on the Internet. Blogs exist on almost any topic, but the anonymity of the Internet often makes checking a blog author's credentials difficult.

Body - The bulk of any research paper, the body consists of everything between the introduction and the conclusion. The body of the paper should lay out the paper's main points and support the thesis statement with cited research.

Boolean search – A type of searching commonly used in search engines and databases. Boolean searches have three primary functions. "And," "Or," and "Not" are used to set the parameters for the search. Using "And" between keywords will return only results that contain both keywords. Using "Or" will return results that contain either keyword. Using "Not" eliminates any results that feature an unwanted term.

Brackets – In research papers, brackets are used to insert words into a quotation. Brackets should be used sparingly and only when additional context is needed for the quote to make sense. They are most commonly used to replace a pronoun with the noun it is referencing when that noun is not otherwise included in the quotation.

Catalog – Used in libraries to organize and allow users to search for particular information. Catalogs used to consist of cards detailing information on each title in the library, but most libraries now employ digital catalogs. These allow users to search more easily and efficiently than they could with card catalogs.

Citation – A notation after a piece of research giving credit to the author or source that the information came from.

Citation guidelines - Several methods exist for citing sources, the three most common formats being MLA, APA, and Chicago/Turabian. These guidelines explain how to cite various sources so they are uniform and easily understood by the reader.

Conclusion - The last section in a paper. Conclusions generally start out by restating the paper's thesis and then broadening from there. The best conclusions will briefly recap the paper's main points while also explaining how they are applicable to the reader and/or the world.

Credibility - The trustworthiness of a source, or how reliable the information contained in a source is. *See Chapter 5 for more details on evaluating credibility.*

Cross-reference - Comparing and contrasting information on a subject from one source to information in a different source. This is a good way of checking the validity and credibility of information.

Database - An organized collection of information on one or more topics, usually in digital form. Databases have largely replaced card catalogs in student research. Academic databases are a great source of articles and other sources for research papers.

Dissertations - A written essay, paper, or other long compilation on a particular topic. This term generally refers to the piece of writing graduate level students write to be awarded a doctorate. These can be great sources for papers, as well as great places to look for other sources pertaining to a particular topic.

Ellipsis – Used in research papers to indicate that something has been omitted from a quotation. They should be used sparingly and should never be used to change the context of a quote, but rather to omit information that is not pertinent to the topic of the paper.

Endnote – A note at the end of a document, generally referenced by a superscript or subscript number within the document.

File – A collection of records or other data, usually digital in nature.

Footnote – An explanatory note or comment at the bottom of the page, usually in reference to a particular piece of information contained on that page.

Foreword – A short introductory statement preceding a published work. These are generally written by someone other than the author.

Glossary – A list of terms and definitions pertaining to a special subject or field of study.

Index – An alphabetical listing of topics found at the end of most books and other long documents. Indexes generally include all page numbers where a particular word, phrase, or topic is mentioned, which makes navigating a long work much simpler.

Interpolate – To introduce new information into a document, or to otherwise alter a document. This term is generally used to indicate deceptive altering of documents or intentional misquoting.

Introduction – A short statement at the beginning of a work that explains what will be covered in the document. Introductions are generally written by the author of the book, article, or paper. This can also refer to the first paragraph of a research paper.

Journal – A periodical, generally published by or for a special group, profession, or organization. This term is sometimes also applied to newspapers, especially daily ones.

Keyword – A significant or defining descriptor in the title, summary, or text of a document.

Pagination – The number of pages in a manuscript, or the way in which a manuscript's pages are marked to indicate their order.

Peer-reviewed article – An article, sometimes called a Refereed article, that was reviewed by other scholars in a field of study before publication.

Periodical – A magazine, newspaper, or other journal that is printed on a regular, periodic schedule.

Plagiarism – The unlawful or unauthorized use of the language, thoughts, or intellectual property of another author. Representing the work of another as though it were your own original work.

Précis – See Abstract.

Preface – An introductory section, generally used in a

book or other longer work, that explains or introduces the topic and gives background information on the topic, author, research, etc. This is usually, but not always, written by someone other than the author of the actual book or article.

Primary source - An original and authoritative document or eyewitness account pertaining to an event or subject.

Refereed article - See Peer-reviewed article.

Review - A critical evaluation of a document, book, or other work.

Rough draft - The first, unpolished version of a piece of writing

Scan - To glance over a document and survey it for important, stand out ideas to get an idea of its content.

Search engine - A program that searches documents, particularly on the Internet, for a keyword, as defined by the user.

Secondary source - Any document that describes an event, subject, place, or thing that was not created at the time of the event or by an eyewitness.

Synopsis - See Abstract.

Thesaurus - A reference book of synonyms and antonyms.

Thesis - A proposition put forward in a research paper or other document that is then defended and argued by the author.

Transition – A word, phrase, sentence, or passage that links an idea or section to the idea or section following it.

Website – A connected group of pages on the Internet, usually devoted to a person, organization, purpose, or topic.

Wikipedia – A well-known Internet-based encyclopedia that allows anyone to add, delete, or revise its content.

Author Biography

 Erika L. Eby is a freelance writer, editor, artist, photographer, and e-book author. A jack-of-all-trades, she holds a degree in English with an emphasis in composition from Carthage College. Her writing experience covers a variety of topics, including opinion pieces, how-to guides, reviews, promotional pieces, and academic research, as well as prose and poetry. Her open and honest approach to writing makes her pieces easy to understand and relate to. She resides in Racine, Wisconsin. You can visit her through her website at **www.hijINKSstudios.com** or by emailing her at MsErikaEby@gmail.com.

Index